I0428075

AFTER PARIS AND COPENHAGEN: RESPONDING TO THE RISING TIDE OF ANTI-SEMITISM

HEARING

BEFORE THE

SUBCOMMITTEE ON AFRICA, GLOBAL HEALTH, GLOBAL HUMAN RIGHTS, AND INTERNATIONAL ORGANIZATIONS

OF THE

COMMITTEE ON FOREIGN AFFAIRS
HOUSE OF REPRESENTATIVES

ONE HUNDRED FOURTEENTH CONGRESS

FIRST SESSION

_____

MARCH 24, 2015

_____

Serial No. 114–28

_____

Printed for the use of the Committee on Foreign Affairs

Available via the World Wide Web: http://www.foreignaffairs.house.gov/ or http://www.gpo.gov/fdsys/

_____

U.S. GOVERNMENT PUBLISHING OFFICE

93–914PDF   WASHINGTON : 2015

_____

For sale by the Superintendent of Documents, U.S. Government Publishing Office
Internet: bookstore.gpo.gov   Phone: toll free (866) 512–1800; DC area (202) 512–1800
Fax: (202) 512–2104   Mail: Stop IDCC, Washington, DC 20402–0001

COMMITTEE ON FOREIGN AFFAIRS

EDWARD R. ROYCE, California, *Chairman*

CHRISTOPHER H. SMITH, New Jersey
ILEANA ROS-LEHTINEN, Florida
DANA ROHRABACHER, California
STEVE CHABOT, Ohio
JOE WILSON, South Carolina
MICHAEL T. McCAUL, Texas
TED POE, Texas
MATT SALMON, Arizona
DARRELL E. ISSA, California
TOM MARINO, Pennsylvania
JEFF DUNCAN, South Carolina
MO BROOKS, Alabama
PAUL COOK, California
RANDY K. WEBER SR., Texas
SCOTT PERRY, Pennsylvania
RON DeSANTIS, Florida
MARK MEADOWS, North Carolina
TED S. YOHO, Florida
CURT CLAWSON, Florida
SCOTT DesJARLAIS, Tennessee
REID J. RIBBLE, Wisconsin
DAVID A. TROTT, Michigan
LEE M. ZELDIN, New York
TOM EMMER, Minnesota

ELIOT L. ENGEL, New York
BRAD SHERMAN, California
GREGORY W. MEEKS, New York
ALBIO SIRES, New Jersey
GERALD E. CONNOLLY, Virginia
THEODORE E. DEUTCH, Florida
BRIAN HIGGINS, New York
KAREN BASS, California
WILLIAM KEATING, Massachusetts
DAVID CICILLINE, Rhode Island
ALAN GRAYSON, Florida
AMI BERA, California
ALAN S. LOWENTHAL, California
GRACE MENG, New York
LOIS FRANKEL, Florida
TULSI GABBARD, Hawaii
JOAQUIN CASTRO, Texas
ROBIN L. KELLY, Illinois
BRENDAN F. BOYLE, Pennsylvania

AMY PORTER, *Chief of Staff*   THOMAS SHEEHY, *Staff Director*

JASON STEINBAUM, *Democratic Staff Director*

––––––––

SUBCOMMITTEE ON AFRICA, GLOBAL HEALTH, GLOBAL HUMAN RIGHTS, AND INTERNATIONAL ORGANIZATIONS

CHRISTOPHER H. SMITH, New Jersey, *Chairman*

MARK MEADOWS, North Carolina
CURT CLAWSON, Florida
SCOTT DesJARLAIS, Tennessee
TOM EMMER, Minnesota

KAREN BASS, California
DAVID CICILLINE, Rhode Island
AMI BERA, California

CONTENTS

(III)

AFTER PARIS AND COPENHAGEN: RESPONDING TO THE RISING TIDE OF ANTI–SEMITISM

TUESDAY, MARCH 24, 2015

HOUSE OF REPRESENTATIVES,
SUBCOMMITTEE ON AFRICA, GLOBAL HEALTH,
GLOBAL HUMAN RIGHTS, AND INTERNATIONAL ORGANIZATIONS,
COMMITTEE ON FOREIGN AFFAIRS,
Washington, DC.

The subcommittee met, pursuant to notice, at 2:43 p.m., in room 2175 Rayburn House Office Building, Hon. Christopher H. Smith (chairman of the subcommittee) presiding.

Mr. SMITH. The subcommittee will come to order. Good afternoon and welcome to everyone joining us today. I particularly want to welcome our witnesses and Ambassador Ronald Lauder, the president of the World Jewish Congress; Mr. Roger Cukierman, president of the Representative Council of Jewish Institutions of France; and Mr. Dan Asmussen, chairperson of the Danish Jewish Community.

In 1982, during my first term in Congress, I traveled with the National Conference on Soviet Jewry to Moscow and Leningrad, now St. Petersburg, to meet with Jewish refusniks in their homes and to engage Soviet leaders. Mark Levin invited me to be on that trip and has been a friend and a mentor ever since. For hours on end, Mark and I and a delegation that included former Democrat member of this committee, who was a ranking member, Sam Gejdenson, heard stories of the Soviets' physical and mental abuse, systemic harassment, gulags and psychiatric prisons, and an array of similarly wanton and brutal acts of anti-Semitism.

To apply for an exit visa, a universally recognized human right, which on paper, at least, the Soviet Union had acceded to, was to invite the cruelty and the wrath of the KGB and other small minded, morally stunted thugs. To courageously seek freedom rendered you ineligible for employment in Lenin's farcical workers' paradise. The Soviet system, militantly atheistic and morally incoherent, wouldn't let Jews leave, but didn't want Jews to stay either, a bizarre paradox.

To a brand new, 27-year-old Congressman, it was bewildering and deeply troubling. Why do they hate Jews? And I pondered that question over and over again and why the anti-Semitic obsession? Well, sadly, it has not changed and it is getting worse.

This is the ninth hearing I have chaired on combating anti-Semitism. The first was right after the Republicans took control. We put together a hearing called ''The Rising Tide of Anti-Semitism.'' And even though the Soviet Union had matriculated to Russia, we heard how anti-Semitism had become privatized and the government was doing little or nothing to mitigate its occurrence. We also heard that it was rising everywhere as well.

However, never in modern times has the need to defend Jews everywhere been greater. Our next hearings will be on the explosion of anti-Semitic hate on college campuses and Jewish community security which increasingly has to be addressed and real dollars put in place to lessen that threat as well.

For the first time since the Holocaust, the physical security of Jewish communities in Europe have become a top level concern. Our hearing today will examine the horrifying state of affairs facing Jewish communities in Europe at this time.

At a congressional hearing that I had in 2002, Dr. Shimon Samuels of the Wiesenthal Center in Paris testified and I quote him, ''The Holocaust for 30 years after the war acted as a protective teflon against blatant anti-Semitic expression, especially in Europe. That teflon,'' he said, ''has eroded and what was considered distasteful and politically incorrect is becoming simply an opinion. But cocktail chatter,'' he went on to say, ''at fine English dinners can end as Molotov cocktails against synagogues.''

That is exactly where we are now, 13 years later. What was anti-Semitic cocktail chatter then, has now led to two people shot and killed at a synagogue and a Jewish cultural center in Copenhagen and four killed in a terrorist attack on a kosher supermarket in Paris. These are only the most recent outrages in a terrifying increase of extreme anti-Semitic violence. Let us not forget the May 2014 murder of four people at the Jewish Museum in Brussels and the March 2012 murder of three Jewish children and a rabbi at a Jewish school in the French city of Toulouse.

Each of these four attacks was perpetrated by a killer who has links to a jihadist movement. For far too long, far too many government officials, many of them mired in what Natan Sharansky summarized as ''the application of double standards and the demonization of Israel'' have reacted weakly to this danger. Meanwhile, the threat has grown exponentially.

Today, at least 3,000, perhaps more than 5,000 EU citizens have left to join ISIS in Syria, Iraq, and other conflict zones. This is the recent estimates of Europol, the EU's joint criminal intelligence body. It would be criminally irresponsible not to take this number as a warning of events much worse to come and to make every effort to prepare accordingly. And of course, that also applies to those who have gone to those battlefields from the United States.

In 2002, in response to what appeared to be a sudden frightening spike in anti-Semitism in several countries including the U.S., I first proposed the idea of conferences on combating anti-Semitism under the auspices of the Organization for Security and Co-operation in Europe. Convinced we had an escalating crisis on our hands, I teamed with several OSCE partners, including Germany and members of the Bundestag, to push for action and reform. Many of the people in the NGOs present in this room played leading and pivotal roles in that effort. Those efforts directly led to the creation of the OSCE Chairperson-in-Office's Personal Representative on Combating Anti-Semitism, which has been filled with great distinction by Rabbi Andy Baker since 2009.

Rabbi Baker has done outstanding work, dogged and energetic. He has been the driver behind everything the OSCE has done, has accomplished in fighting anti-Semitism in recent years.

My efforts with partners to put anti-Semitism on the OSCE agenda also led to important conferences in Vienna, Berlin, in Bucharest, and last fall in Berlin. In each of these, participating states have made solemn, tangible commitments to put our words into action. In some countries progress indeed has been made. Institutions that fight anti-Semitism have been created and they have done excellent work. They have also done the all-important work of chronicling it. As Sharansky said at one of our hearings, "If you don't chronicle the crime, how can you fight it?" But it has not been enough to reverse the new anti-Semitism sweeping Europe and it has failed miserably to anticipate and prevent the arrival of jihadist anti-Semitism in Europe. That is why we are here today, to review, recommit, and reenergize efforts to stop the evil of anti-Semitic violence that is threatening the Jewish communities of Europe. And again, this is worldwide, but our focus primarily is on Europe today.

We need to learn more about what must be done to ensure community security, how the community sees the threats they face, what they are doing about them, what the European governments are doing about them and how everyone can and must do more.

We can also learn how the U.S. should do more and be more effective in this fight. And this is especially in light of World Jewish Congress President Lauder's all-important question, who will lead off our witnesses, when he says in testimony today, "Where is the United States?" Ambassador Lauder will say, "Once again, like the 1930s, European Jews live in fear. In my travels to all of these communities," he goes on, "I am asked the question around Europe and the world. Where is the United States? Why isn't the United States leading the world in this crisis?"

I would like to now yield to my good friend and colleague, Mr. Mark Meadows, for any comments he might have.

Mr. MEADOWS. Thank you, Mr. Chairman, and thank each of you for being here and also thank you to the 60 or so of you who are here from the World Jewish Congress. I noticed that you were here because you were arguing with each other on which way to get to the hearing room and it is a pleasure to have you here.

Sadly, this is an all too familiar theme and what we have heard and I will speak from the heart today because for this particular issue, it is a passion for me. It is one that we must continue to not only voice and articulate, but do it in a way that is persuasive where we can bring the rest of the world to an understanding of what happens each and every day. And I say each and every day because there are over 550 violent anti-Semitic crimes that are perpetrated every year. And so when we look at that and I am not just talking about slights, I am talking about violent incidents, so almost two a day, that are being experienced across the country and across the world.

And when we look at that, to put it in context, we have not seen this level since the days of World War II. And when we look at that, it is troubling when we can see that kind of rhetoric, hostility, and truly a hatred that continues to come out and honestly be justified because of some action that is happening somewhere else. To think that this would be an action that could somehow be justified because of a political, geopolitical thing that is happening throughout the world is inexcusable.

But I also think that it is critical for us to continue to raise the awareness. There is a generation that is coming up that do not know from history other than reading in textbooks what happened during World War II. It is not personal. The Holocaust survivors are truly disappearing at an alarming rate just because of age and yet, we are not doing a good job of truly educating and informing the generation to come.

And so my plea to each one of you is as Chairman Smith raises this issue in this hearing and the witness testimony hopefully will highlight it today, is that I need you to redouble your effort in your communities, in your synagogues, in the places where you do business, to make sure that this message continues to get told to the generations that are coming.

I will close with this. It is a personal story of my wife and I on the banks of a river in Budapest and there on the banks are some shoes, some bronze shoes. They are a reminder of a terrible, terrible thing that happened long ago. And yet, if we do not stand firm today, that same tragedy could happen again, and in ways is happening again today. And so I look forward to the testimony and I join the chairman in an unyielding resolve to make sure that we address this particular issue. And I thank the chairman.

Mr. SMITH. Mr. Meadows, thank you very much for your opening comments and thank you for your leadership. I would note for the record that Mr. Meadows is not only one of the leaders on religious freedom in general, believing that we all need to protect the rights of people of faith to act and believe and follow their conscience, but he has been especially tenacious on the issue of combating anti-Semitism and I want to thank him for that.

I would like to recognize our distinguished witnesses beginning first with Ambassador Ronald Lauder, who has served as President of the World Jewish Congress since June 2007 and has championed the safety and security of the State of Israel in the public arena for many years. From 1983 to 1986, he served as Deputy Assistant Secretary of Defense for European and NATO Affairs. And in 1986, he was appointed by President Ronald Reagan as Ambassador to Austria. He is the former chairman of the Conference of Presidents of Major American-Jewish Organizations and has made the fight against anti-Semitism a life-long endeavor. He is a man who has truly made a difference.

We will then hear from Mr. Roger Cukierman who was elected as President of the Representative Council of Jewish Institutions of France in 2001. He was reelected in 2004 and again in 2013. He is Vice President of the World Jewish Congress and serves as Treasurer of the Foundation for the Memory of the Shoah. He is active in many of the social and educational institutions of the Jewish community and has made the fight against anti-Semitism his main priority, demanding French Government action to fight hate crimes, defending the safety and security of Jewish schools, houses of worship, and urging solidarity with victims of terror.

We will then hear from Mr. Dan Rosenberg Asmussen who was elected as the chairperson of the Danish Jewish Community Center in 2014. In his professional career, he is the Deputy Director of the Association of Danish Pharmacies. He played an important role in the immediate aftermath of the attack at the Copenhagen synagogue last month by managing the crisis unit and liaisoning with local law enforcement authorities as well as political leaders.

So Ambassador Lauder, if you could begin your statement.

STATEMENT OF THE HONORABLE RONALD S. LAUDER, PRESIDENT, WORLD JEWISH CONGRESS

Ambassador LAUDER. Thank you very much, Mr. Chairman. But before I start, Mr. Meadows mentioned the shoes along the Danube. What had happened in the closing days of World War II, as the Russians were surrounding Budapest and they cut off the rail lines, they still wanted to kill more Jewish people. They took something like 5,000 Jewish people, had them undress, put 10 and 20 together, roped together with wire and pushed them into the Danube and let them drown together, just as a last ditch effort to kill people. It was the Arrow Cross that did most of it and interestingly enough the Arrow Cross has been re-erected in Budapest and it is now an organization there with a terrible history. Thank you.

I would like to thank you personally, Mr. Chairman, for your support of every religion, race, gender, and age who live in this great country.

The particular topic today at this particular moment in history after Paris and Copenhagen, responding to the rising tide of anti-Semitism, is sadly all too timely. It is reminiscent of an even darker age that we thought was behind us. With your permission, I would like to submit a statement.

Exactly 70 years ago, as American GIs advanced into Nazi Germany in the last days of the most devastating war in history, the world had a glimpse of the horror of unbridled anti-Semitism. The images of the concentration camps that were liberated throughout Europe in the spring of 1945 still cause a universal shudder to this day. For the first few decades after World War II, we mistakenly, all of us, believed that anti-Semitism, the age-old hatred of Jews, had finally disappeared from Europe and everywhere else. That is because in the 1950s and 1960s, no one in their right minds wanted to be associated with Nazis. It is because we all saw where this kind of hatred leads. And, perhaps, people who still harbored these beliefs were too embarrassed to express them openly.

I now tell you with the greatest sadness that 70 years later, the age-old virus of anti-Semitism has returned in all its evil and ugliness. Anti-Semitism has returned to streets of Paris and Toulouse, to the streets Brussels and Copenhagen. It has even returned to Berlin.

You will hear the personal accounts from my friend, Roger Cukierman, the head of the Jewish community in Paris, but listen to these frightening facts.

Jews make up less than 1 percent of the population of France, but they were victims of more than half of all the racial attacks in that country last year. The number of anti-Jewish attacks in France in 2014 doubled from the year before. In Great Britain, the number of anti-Semitic attacks also doubled from the year before. In Austria, again we saw the amount of anti-Semitic attacks doubling. In fact, the EU report from 9 nations showed that 16 months ago, long before the latest wave of terror, Jews in these countries were already concerned about growing anti-Semitism. You don't have to be a mathematician to see an obvious trend here.

There is a hatred growing throughout Europe that is causing Jews to wonder if they should leave. They are asking if there is a future for Jews on that continent.

Last fall, I sat with representatives of the Jewish community in Rome and they told me that although they may stay, their children and definitely their grandchildren will leave. They told me that the Jewish community in Rome, that has existed since the time of Christ and survived Hitler, would disappear within 25 years. How could this happen in 2015?

The answer is that a strange confluence of hatred has taken hold across Europe today that comes from many different corners. There are huge populations of Muslim immigrants throughout Europe. Most are peaceful, but far too many of them have adopted radical Islam. There are thousands of young European Muslims that have left to fight with Islamic radicals in Iraq and Syria, and there is a real fear that they could return, bringing the bloodshed with them. Some have already returned and we have seen the consequences.

At the same time, we have seen the rise of smaller right wing Neo-Nazi extremist groups that have become political forces in Hungary and Greece and have been seen on the streets in Germany and France. And there is a third force that may appear more benign, but it adds fuel to this fire. I am talking about an educated, elitist class, from universities to the media, that has a pathological hatred of Israel. They would never consider themselves anti-Semitic, but they are quite open in their opinion that only Israel is the source of all of the problems in the Middle East. This is intellectually dishonest and devoid of reality. But too many people have accepted their lies as the truth.

And then there is technology. Seventy years ago, Josef Goebbels used newspapers, film, and marches to infuse hatred of Jews into mainstream society. Today, the power of the Internet sends out a constant stream of anti-Semitic ideas at hyperspeed and there are not enough people speaking up to counter these lies.

Do you want to know what it is like to be openly Jewish in Europe today? Just go to YouTube and watch what happens when a young man simply walks down a European street wearing a yarmulke. He is insulted, shoved, spat on, and as we saw in France, Jews who are openly Jewish can also be killed.

Once again, like the 1930s, many European Jews live in fear.

Members of the committee, in my travels to all of the communities, I am asked the same question around Europe and the world, I have been asked where is the United States? Why isn't the United States leading the world in that crisis? Right after the attacks on Charlie Hebdo and the kosher grocery store in Paris, over 1 million people marched in defiance of those murders. Many of the leaders of Europe linked arms in solidarity in the very front row. But there was not one U.S. representative with them in the front row.

I believe this sent a very negative message around the world. European leaders have stepped up and strongly condemned these attacks on Jews and the rise of anti-Semitism. The United States must do the same. The United States must lead. When a Neo-Nazi party like Jobbik in Hungary or Golden Dawn in Greece wins substantial votes in elections, the United States must condemn in the strongest possible terms these anti-Semitic parties. My fear is that muted condemnations or worse, silence, could lead to what we saw in Europe 70 years ago. and that led to deaths of 60 million people and the destruction of a continent.

We must insist that European nations better share intelligence on anti-Semitic Islamic hate preachers. All countries must better monitor radical Islam recruiting in prisons, on the Internet, and in mosques. And without question, we must closely monitor European and U.S. nationals returning from the Middle East and Africa. The United States can and must speak loudly and clearly to condemn this evil for what it is, the radical Islamic hatred of Jews.

Mr. Chairman, one of the bravest men in history, Sir Winston Churchill, came to Westminster College in Fulton, Missouri in 1946 and he warned us that the Soviet takeover of Eastern Europe was complete and an Iron Curtain had descended across the continent. Churchill was trying to wake up a sleeping world because too many people didn't want to believe him. We had just fought a war against totalitarianism and we were tired. We didn't want to fight another one.

Well, today, it is not an Iron Curtain that is descending across Eastern Europe. It is a white-hot fire and its reach is much greater. This new, incandescent flame is scorching the entire Middle East from Tehran, across Iraq, and through Syria, Lebanon, Gaza, and now Yemen. It stretches across parts of North Africa. It destroys everything in its path and leaves nothing alive, not Jews, not Christians and not Muslims who don't share their exact beliefs.

Unless we act now, the flame of radical Islam could stretch across all of Europe as well. After Churchill's speech in Missouri, it took 44 years and billions of dollars to defeat Soviet Communism. We were focused back then, we were committed, we were united with our allies, and we were able to win the Cold War without horrific bloodshed.

But in order to defeat this new flame of radical Islamic terror and survive, the United States must lead. I fear that if we do not stand up to this new foe immediately, it will take us much longer than 44 years to defeat it. I fear it will cost us much more of our treasure and, most tragically of all, I fear it will consume many, many more lives, not just in the Middle East and Europe, but here as well.

Members of the committee, we must not let this happen again. Thank you.

[The prepared statement of Ambassador Lauder follows:]

Congressional Testimony of Ronald Lauder
President
World Jewish Congress
March 24, 2015

Mr. Chairman, my name is Ronald Lauder.
I live in New York City and I am the President of the World Jewish Congress, the international organization that represents Jewish communities in 100 countries around the world.

Before I begin, I would like to personally thank you for your many years of support to the Jewish community as well as your support for people of all religions, races, genders and age who live in our great country.

This particular topic, at this particular moment in history, ***After Paris and Copenhagen, Responding to the Rising Tide Of Anti-Semitism*** is, sadly, all too timely … and it is reminiscent of an even darker time that we thought was behind us.

With your permission, I would like to submit my opening statement for the record.

Statement:

Exactly 70 years ago, as American G.I.s advanced into Nazi-Germany in the last days of the most devastating war in history, the world saw its first glimpse of the horror of unbridled anti-Semitism.

The images of the concentration camps that were liberated throughout Europe in the spring of 1945 still cause a universal shudder to this day.

For the first few decades following World War II, we mistakenly believed that anti-Semitism – the age-old hatred of Jews – had finally disappeared from Europe and everywhere else.

That is because in the 1950s and 1960s, no one in their right minds wanted to be associated with Nazis.

It is because we all saw where this kind of hatred leads.

And, perhaps, people who still harbored these beliefs were too embarrassed to express them openly.

I now tell you with the greatest sadness that 70 years later, the age-old virus of anti-Semitism has returned in all its evil and ugliness.

Anti-Semitism has returned to streets of Paris and Toulouse … to the streets of

Brussels and Copenhagen ... it has even returned to Berlin.

(You will hear the personal accounts from my friend, Roger Cukierman, the head of the Jewish community in Paris, but listen to these frightening facts.)

Jews make up less than one percent of the population of France but they were victims of more than half of all the racist attacks in that country last year.

The number of anti-Jewish attacks in France in 2014 doubled from the year before.

In Great Britain, the number of anti-Semitic attacks doubled from the year before.

In Austria, anti-Semitic attacks doubled from the year before.

In fact, an EU report from nine nations showed that 16 months ago – long before the latest wave of terror – Jews in these countries were already concerned about growing anti-Semitism.

You don't have to be a mathematician to see an obvious trend here.

There is a hatred growing throughout Europe that is causing Jews to wonder if they should leave ... they are asking if there is a future for Jews on that continent.

Last fall, I sat with representatives of the Jewish community in Rome and they told me that although they may stay ... their children and definitely their grandchildren will leave. They told me that the Jewish community in Rome, that has existed since the time of Christ and survived Hitler, would disappear within 25 years.

How could this happen in 2015?

The answer is that a strange confluence of hatred has taken hold across Europe today that comes from very different corners.

There are huge populations of Muslim immigrants throughout Europe. Most are peaceful, but far too many of them have adopted radical Islam.

There are thousands of young European Muslims that have left to fight with Islamic radicals in Iraq and Syria, and there is a real fear that they could return, bringing the bloodshed with them.

Some have already returned and we have seen the consequences.

At the same time, we have seen the rise of smaller right wing Neo-Nazi extremist groups that have become political forces in Hungary and Greece and have been seen on the streets in Germany and France.

And there is a third force that may appear more benign, but it adds fuel to this fire. I'm talking about an educated, elitist class – from universities to the media – that has a pathological hatred of Israel.

They would never consider themselves anti-Semitic but they are quite open in their opinion that only Israel is the source of all of the problems in the Middle East.

This is intellectually dishonest and devoid of reality. But too many people have accepted their lies as the truth.

And then there is technology.

70 years ago, Josef Goebbels used newspapers, film and marches to infuse hatred of Jews into mainstream society.

Today, the power of the internet sends out a constant stream of anti-Jewish ideas at hyperspeed .. and there are not enough people speaking up to counter these lies.

Do you want to know what it's like to be openly Jewish in Europe today?

Just go to YouTube and watch what happens when a young man simply walks down a European street wearing a yarmulke.

He is insulted ... shoved ... spat on ... and as we saw in France ... Jews who are openly Jewish can also be killed.

Once again, like the 1930s, European Jews live in fear.

Members of the Committee ...

In my travels to all of these communities, I am asked the same question around Europe and the world:

Where is the United States?

Why isn't the United States leading the world in this crisis?

Right after the attacks on Charlie Hebdo and the Kosher grocery store in Paris ... over 1-million people marched in defiance of those murders.

Many of the leaders in Europe linked arms in solidarity in the very front row ...

but there was not one U.S. representative with them in the front row.

I believe that sent a very negative message around the world.

European leaders have stepped up and strongly condemned these attacks on Jews and the rise of anti-Semitism.

The United States must do the same.

The United States must lead.

When a Neo-Nazi party like Jobik in Hungary or Golden Dawn in Greece wins substantial seats in elections ... the United States must condemn this in the strongest possible terms.

My fear is that muted condemnations or, worse, silence, could lead to what we saw in Europe 70 years ago ... and that led to deaths of 60 million people and the destruction of a continent.

We must insist that European nations better share intelligence on anti-Semitic Islamic hate preachers ... all countries must better monitor radical Islamic recruiting in prisons, on the internet and in mosques ... and without question, we must closely monitor European and U.S. nationals returning from the Middle East and Africa.

The United States can and must speak loudly and clearly to condemn this evil for what it is – the radical Islamic hatred of Jews.

Mr. Chairman, one of the bravest men in history, Sir Winston Churchill, came to Westminster College in Fulton, Missouri in 1946 and warned us that the Soviet takeover of Eastern Europe was complete and an Iron Curtain had descended across the continent.

Churchill was trying to wake up a sleeping world because too many people didn't want to believe him.

We had just fought a war against totalitarianism and we were tired ... we didn't want to fight another one.

Well, today, it's not an Iron Curtain that is descending across Eastern Europe ... it is a white-hot fire and its reach is much greater.

This new, incandescent flame is scorching the entire Middle East from Tehran across Iraq and through Syria, Lebanon, Gaza and now Yemen.

It stretches across parts of Northern Africa.

It destroys everything in its path and leaves nothing alive ... not Jews, not Christians and not Muslims who don't share their exact beliefs.

Unless we act right now, the flame of radical Islam could stretch across all of Europe as well.

After Churchill's speech in Missouri, it took 44 years and billions of dollars to defeat Soviet Communism.

We were focused back then, we were committed, we were united with our allies and we were able to win the Cold War without horrific bloodshed.

But in order to defeat this new flame of radical Islamic terror and survive ... the United States must lead.

I fear that if we do not stand up to this new foe immediately, it will take us much longer than 44 years to defeat it.

I fear it will cost us much more of our treasure and, most tragically of all, I fear it will consume many, many more lives – not just in the Middle East and Europe ... but here as well.

Members of the Committee, we must NOT let this happen again.

Thank you.

Mr. Smith. Ambassador Lauder, thank you very much for your very powerful and sobering comments to the subcommittee and by extension to the Congress and to the American people, thank you.

I would like to now recognize Mr. Roger Cukierman.

STATEMENT OF MR. ROGER CUKIERMAN, PRESIDENT, REPRESENTATIVE COUNCIL OF JEWISH INSTITUTIONS OF FRANCE

Mr. Cukierman. Mr. Chairman, members of the committee, thank you for the opportunity to appear before this subcommittee.

Jews have lived in France for the last 2,000 years. One thousand years ago, at the time of the crusades, the famous Talmudist Rachi was living in the city of Troyes. He was producing wine, a typical French job, and he was also famous for his expertise in old French language. More than 200 years ago in 1791, at the time of the French Revolution, French Jews were given full French citizenship. Today, we are ½ million Jews in France, less than 1 percent of the French population. And the CRIF which I chair is the roof body of French Jewish institutions. It is comparable to the President's Conference of Major Jewish Institutions.

Today, in 2015, our synagogues and our Jewish schools have to be protected by the police and even by the army with machine guns. Why is that so? Because there is a World War started by Middle Age barbarian fanatics who are cutting heads, are stoning women, are killing kids, and want to impose to the rest of the world the Sharia, their concept of what Islam should be in their views.

The first victims are the moderate Muslims. This is a war against Western modern civilization. And the Jews are seen by these jihadists as a privileged target. We Jews are the sentinels at the forefront of this war. But we are not the only victims. Military forces, policemen and women, and journalists are also targeted and killed. These jihadists are acting under different names: Daesh, ISIS, al-Qaeda, Boko Haram, AQIM, Hamas. It started in the Middle East: Syria, Iraq, Yemen, and Gaza. It reaches Africa: Mali, Niger, Nigeria, Cameroon, Chad, and Tunisia and now it is in Europe: France, Belgium, and Denmark.

In France, small children were killed in March 2012 in Toulouse, at point-blank at the entrance of a school by Mohamed Merah. In 2014, four people were killed in the Jewish Museum of Brussels by Mehdi Nemouche. And then in January 2015, four people were killed in the Paris kosher grocery store, and then in front of the Copenhagen Synagogue. All victims were targeted because they were Jews. All these killers were jihadists.

In front of that situation the French Government shows a perfect understanding of our situation. Prime Minister Manuel Valls said that anti-Zionism is anti-Semitism. And President Hollande said that ''it is not the Jews who should leave the country, it is the anti-Semites.'' And immediately after the grocery attack, the government added close to 8,000 military to the police forces to protect the Jewish places.

From where are these jihadists coming? They come from the Muslim community which is estimated in France around 10 percent of the total French population. And the French jihadists is estimated at 1,300 people who are presently combating in Syria and Iraq. And among them many French ethnics recently converted to Islam.

It seems that they are generally not influenced by the French imams, not influenced by the press which they don't read, nor by the TV that they don't watch. They were educated to the jihad in the French jails and by Internet.

This is why the CRIF, our organization, bought a full page ad in the New York Times on March 2, 2015, which was an appeal to our American friends and also to you asking that they should put pressure on the Internet providers to set a limit to the swarm of hate which can be found on Internet, to remove anti-Semitic contents as soon as it is flagged. On the Internet ways were found to ban child pornography. Likewise anti-Semitism must be banned. The providers of Internet must understand that they bear a responsibility when murders are committed by youngsters who became jihadists through Internet.

Now the question that I am asked daily is whether there a future for Jews in France?

An increasing number of French Jews are considering leaving France. The French Jewish population which is estimated at ½ million people, is the third largest Jewish community in the world after Israel and the U.S. In the last 3 years, 12,000 French citizens left to Israel. Others chose the U.S., Canada, or Australia. Many people refuse to see the future of their kids if they have to study in schools or to go to synagogues which appear as fortresses protected by military and heavy machine guns. The atmosphere is tense. One cannot travel in the subway with a yarmulke. Anti-Semitism is active in many suburbs and in many public schools.

Nevertheless, I believe that a big proportion of the French Jews will remain in France where their roots and their culture incite them to confront adversity as their parents or ancestors did at difficult periods like the Dreyfus Affair or the Vichy period.

Thank you and I am, of course, ready to answer any questions.

[The prepared statement of Mr. Cukierman follows:]

Testimony to the House of Representatives

By Roger Cukierman Chairman of CRIF

Jews have lived in France for the last 2.000 years. One thousand years ago, at the time of the crusades, the famous Talmudist Rachi was living in the city of Troyes. He was producing wine, a typical French job, and he was also famous for his expertise in old French language.

In 1791, at the time of the French revolution, French Jews were given the full French citizenship.

And today, in 2015, our synagogues and our Jewish schools have to be protected by the police and even the army with machine guns.

Why ?

Because there is a World War started by middle age barbarian fanatics who are cutting heads, are stoning women, are killing kids, and want to impose to the rest of the world the Sharia, their concept of what Islam should be in their views.

The first victims are the moderate Muslims. This is a war against western modern civilization. And the Jews are seen by these Jihadists as a privileged target. We Jews are the sentinels at the forefront of this war. But we are not the only victims. Military forces, policemen and women, journalists were also targeted and killed.

These Jihadists are acting under different names: Daesh, Al Qaida, Boko Haram, Aqmi, Hamas. It started in the Middle East: Syria, Iraq, Yemen, Gaza... It reached Africa: Mali, Niger, Nigeria, Cameroun, Chad, Tunisia... And now Europe: France, Belgium, Denmark.

In France small children were killed in March 2012 in Toulouse, at blank point at the entrance of a school of Otzar hatorah by Mohamed Merah. In 2014, 4 people were killed in the Jewish museum by Mehdi Nemouche. And then in January 2015, 4 people were killed in the Paris kosher grocery store. And then in front of the Copenhagen synagogue. All victims were targeted because they were Jews. All these killers were Jihadists.

In front of that situation the French government shows a perfect understanding of our situation. Prime Minister Manuel Valls said that anti-Zionism is anti-Semitism. And President Hollande said that "it is not the Jews who should leave the country, it is the anti-Semites".

And immediately after the grocery attack the Government added 7.500 military to the Police forces to protect the Jewish places.

From where are these Jihadists coming ?

They come from the Muslim community which is estimated to five or six million people in France. The number of French Jihadists is estimated at 1.300 people who are combatting in Syria and Iraq. Among them many French ethnics recently converted to Islam.

It seems that they are generally not influenced by the French Imams, or by the press which they don't read, or by the TV that they don't watch.

They were educated to the Jihad in the French jails and by internet.

This is why our organization bought a full page ad in the New York Times on the 2nd of march 2015 which was an appeal to our American friends asking them to put pressure on the Internet providers to set a limit to the swarm of hate which can be found on Internet, to remove anti-Semitic contents as soon as it is flagged. On the internet ways were found to ban child pornography. Likewise anti-Semitism must be banned. The providers of Internet must understand that they bear a responsibility when murders are committed by youngsters who became Jihadists through Internet.

Is there a future for Jews in France ?

An increasing number of French Jews are considering leaving France. The French Jewish population is estimated at half a million people, third Jewish Community in the world after Israel and the US.

In the last 3 years 12.000 left to Israel. Other chose the US, Canada, Australia. Many people refuse to see the future of their kids if they have to study in schools or to go to synagogues which appear as fortresses protected by military and heavy gun machines. The atmosphere is tense. One cannot travel in the subway with a yarmulke. Anti-Semitism is active in many suburbs and in public schools.

Nevertheless I believe that a big proportion of the French Jews will remain in France were their roots, their culture incite them to confront adversity as their parents or ancestors did at difficult periods like the Dreyfus Affair or the Vichy period.

March 2015

Mr. SMITH. Mr. Cukierman, thank you very much for your insights and counsel and your historical perspective which is very, very illuminating. We look forward to questions when we get to that point.

I would like to now ask Mr. Asmussen, if you would proceed.

STATEMENT OF MR. DAN ROSENBERG ASMUSSEN, PRESIDENT, DANISH JEWISH COMMUNITY

Mr. ASMUSSEN. Dear Mr. Chairman, dear Members of Congress. It is a great honor for me to testify before the United States Congress, although it is on a sad occasion.

You probably think of Denmark as a small and peaceful country. And it is basically also the way we think ourselves. We are people of 5.5 million, 5,000 Jews.

Only 2 years ago, October 2013, the Danish society celebrated the 70 years commemoration of the saving of the Danish Jewry from the Nazi onslaught. It was an amazing achievement of the Danish society to stand up, come together and to save its Jewish minority. The Danish population believed that its Jewish neighbors and friends were an integral of the Danish society, making Denmark a country that could rightfully be defined as righteous among the nations.

On February 15th this year, the Danish society once again came together. This time in order to mourn the loss of Dan Uzan, a 37-year-old Jewish man, who was murdered while protecting the guests at a Bat Mitzah party in the Jewish Community Center. Thousands of Danes came together in order to speak out against terror.

While the community was in shock and despair, Danes showed again how much they care for their Jewish citizens. In the days following the attack, thousands of people showed their respect. They laid flowers in front of Copenhagen's synagogue.

So on February 15, the Jewish community and the whole Danish society was brutally awoken to a new reality. We had warned the authorities for years that such an attack like that could happen on Danish soil. We had urged them to take warning signs seriously, while we, the Jewish community in parallel, took it upon ourselves to safeguard our community.

The terror attack against the Jewish community in Denmark did not occur in a vacuum. It did not happen in Copenhagen just by chance. It was, unfortunately, the culmination of years of growing anti-Semitism. It happened in a country where it has become widely acceptable to criticize and question both Israel and Jews with a carelessness that we did not expect or imagine just a few years ago.

During the Gaza conflict last summer, a few hundred people were evacuated by police because police could not guarantee their safety due to aggression from Hamas supporters during a demonstration calling for peace, calling for a two-state solution.

A few days earlier, almost 4,000 people signed a petition urging Danish media not to use journalists with Jewish heritage for coverage of Middle East conflict. Yet, it was not before the Jewish school in Copenhagen was vandalized with graffiti that politicians decided to react and speak out against these incidents.

It is, however, important to understand that the Danish society itself has never been anti-Semitic and that many of the threats facing Danish Jewry, like in the rest of Europe, come from marginalized and radicalized Muslims, and these form, I believe, a small minority of all Muslims in Denmark.

The terrorist who committed the two murders was born and raised in Denmark and used his religion to justify the crime. Unfortunately, it doesn't seem that he is alone with this view. That was demonstrated when more than 700 people participated in his funeral cheering at him.

At this point, four people are jailed, accused of helping him.

On the other end of the spectrum, we have witnessed how Muslim organizations spoke out against hatred and prejudice against a fellow citizen. We truly appreciate that expression of support and we welcome any such initiatives. It is important for me to emphasize that we have good relations with moderate Muslim organizations. We work together on issues of common religious rights.

However, we still need for the Muslim community to do more, to become more outspoken against violence and hatred, to confront hate and prejudices toward Jews.

Danish society can only do so much. The real long-term solution needs to be found inside the Muslim community, and we need them to take more responsibility in speaking out against anti-Semitism and against terror committed in the name of their religion.

In recent weeks, the Jewish community received strong support from the Danish politicians through the media. We believe it served as a wake-up call and we expect that our problems will now be taken more seriously than in the past.

Last week, Ira Forman visited Copenhagen. Ira Forman is a Special Envoy to Monitor and Combat Anti-Semitism. He made it clear to us that the Danish Government in his opinion is not doing enough compared with the European countries to combat anti-Semitism. And he said that it could never be justified that the Jewish community, or any other minority group for that matter, should have to prioritize security over education or ultimately prioritize security over the future of the community.

Mr. Forman is right. If we spend all our resources on security, our children won't have a future. Yet, if we fail to protect our children, Danish Jewry won't have a future either. The parents simply won't send them to the Jewish school.

We need at this point a long-term governmental plan that will keep our community safe as much as possible. The Justice Department has said that such a plan is in the making. And we need the Muslim community to speak out and help in building a democratic, tolerant, and peaceful society. This is the only viable and long-term solution, so we one day will not need to risk the lives of our children in order for them to protect the community as Dan Uzan did.

I feel truly grateful toward the Danish society for standing up for the Jewish minority in these difficult times. I just wish they had done so when we asked for help after the incidents in Toulouse and Brussels.

Thank you, Mr. Chairman.

[The prepared statement of Mr. Asmussen follows:]

Testimony to House of Representatives

By Dan Asmussen

Chairman Jewish Community of Denmark

Dear Mr. Chairman, Dear members of Congress

It's an great honor for me to testify before the United States Congress. I would like to thank the honorable Congressmen and the World Jewish Congress for allowing me to share a few remarks with you.

You probably think of Denmark as a small and peaceful country. And it is basically also the way, we think ourselves.

In October 2013, the entire Danish society came together in order to celebrate the 70th commemoration of the saving of Danish Jewry from the Nazi onslaught. It was an amazing achievement of the Danish society to stand up, come together and to save its Jewish minority. The Danish population believed that its Jewish neighbors and friends were an integral of the their own society, making Denmark *a* country that could rightfully be defined at Righteous Among the Nations.

On February 15th, the Danish society once again came together. This time to mourn the loss of Dan Uzan, a 37-year-old Jewish man, who was murdered while protecting the guests at a Bat Mitzah party in the Jewish Community Center. Thousands of Danes came together order to speak out against terror, hatred and indifference.

While the community was in shock and despair, Danes once again showed how much they care for their Jewish citizens. In the days following the attack, thousands of people showed their respect. They laid flowers in front of Copenhagen's Synagogue.

On February 15th, the Jewish Community and the whole Danish society was brutally awoken to a new reality. We had warned the authorities for years that one day such an attack could happen on Danish soil. We had urged them to take the warning signs seriously, while we in parallel took it upon ourselves to safeguard our community's security.

The terror attack against the Jewish community in Denmark did not occur in a vacuum. It did not happen in Copenhagen just by chance. It was the culmination of years of growing anti-Semitism. It happened in a country where it has become widely acceptable to criticize and question both Israel and Jews with a carelessness that we did not expect or imagine just a few years ago.

During the Gaza War last summer, a few hundred people were evacuated by police as the latter could not guarantee for their safety during a demonstration calling for peace.

A few days earlier, almost 4,000 people signed a petition urging Danish media outlets not to use journalists with Jewish heritage for coverage of the Middle East conflict.

Yet it was not before the Jewish school in Copenhagen was vandalized with graffiti that politicians decided to react and speak out against these incidents.

It is however, important to understand that the Danish society itself is not has never been anti-Semitic and that many of the threats facing Danish Jewry, like in the rest of Europe, come from marginalized and radicalized Muslims – and these form a small minority of all Muslims in Denmark.

The terrorist who committed the two murders was born and raised in Denmark and used his religion and affiliation to Islam to justify the crime. Unfortunately, he is not alone there with his views. That was demonstrated when more than 700 people participated in his funeral.

On the other end of the specter we have witnessed how Muslims organizations spoke out against hatred and prejudices against their fellow Jewish citizens. We truly appreciate that expression of support and we welcome any such initiatives. It is important for me to emphasize that we have good relations with moderate Muslim organizations. We work together on issues of common religious rights.

However, we still need for the Muslim community to do more, to become more outspoken against violence and hatred. To confront hate and prejudices toward Jews.

The Danish society can only do so much. The real long-term solution needs to be found inside the Muslim community, and we need them to take more responsibility in speaking out against anti-Semitism, and against terror committed in the name of Allah.

In recent weeks, the Jewish community received strong support from the Danish politicians and media. We believe it served as a wake-up call, and we expect that our problems will now be taken more seriously now than in the past.

Last week, I met with Ira Forman, the US Special Envoy to Monitor and Combat Anti-Semitism. He made it clear to us that the Danish government is not doing enough compared with other European countries, to combat Anti-Semitism.

And he said that it could never be justified that the Jewish community, or any other minority group for that matter, should have to prioritize security over education, or ultimately prioritize security over the future of the community.

Mr. Forman is right.

If we spend all our resources on security, our children won't have a future.

Yet if we fail to protect our children, Danish Jewry doesn't have a future either.

We need a long-term governmental plan that will keep our community safe as much as possible. The Danish Justice Department has said that such a plan is in the making.

And we need the Muslim community to speak out and help in building a democratic, tolerant and peaceful society. This is the only viable and long-term solution, so we one day will not need to risk the lives of children in order for them to protect the community.

I feel truly grateful towards the Danish society for standing up for their Jewish minority in these difficult times. I just wish they had done so when we asked for help after the incidents in Toulouse and Brussels.

Thank you Mr. Chairman,

Mr. SMITH. Thank you so very much, Mr. Asmussen, for your statement and insights. We have been joined by some members who weren't here during opening statements so before going to questions, I would like to briefly ask if they would like to give an opening, beginning with David Cicilline who is the acting ranking member.

Mr. CICILLINE. Thank you, Mr. Chairman. I want to thank you for your leadership and for calling today's hearing on responding to the rising tide of anti-Semitism, to give us an opportunity examine in depth, the alarming increase in anti-Semitic incidents in Europe and begin to discuss what approaches should be used to temper this extremism that is unprecedented since the end of World War II.

I would also like to thank our very distinguished witnesses for being here today. Thank you for sharing your assessment of what the current status of anti-Semitism is in Europe and what specific trends you are seeing and what should be done to combat it and how we in Congress can assist.

The rise of anti-Semitism and related hate crimes in recent months is beyond debate. While many were awakened to this reality in January when four Jewish customers were killed in a kosher market in Paris, days after the attack on the satirical magazine, Charlie Hebdo, that left 12 people dead, anti-Semitism has been on the rise since the early 2000s. The United Kingdom last year, for example, recorded the highest number of anti-Semitic incidents with the London police reporting an increase of 120 percent in anti-Semitic crimes in 2014. Most alarming perhaps are recent statistics from the Anti-Defamation League that show that an average of 24 percent of those surveyed in Western European countries harbor some degree of anti-Semitic sentiment with that number jumping much higher in countries like Greece and France.

Furthermore, 66 percent of Jewish respondents indicated that anti-Semitism was a major problem in their respective countries. In response to the tragic attack in Denmark where two individuals were murdered at a synagogue in February, the Israeli Prime Minister stated, ''We are preparing and calling for the absorption of mass immigration from Europe. To the Jews of Europe and to the Jews of the world I say that Israel is waiting for you with open arms.''

The Chief Rabbi of Copenhagen, however, responded, ''We will not let terror dictate our lives. We will not. We will continue living as Jews here in Denmark and everywhere else in the world.''

The environment that is increasingly conductive to anti-Semite must be dealt with head on and immediately stopped. The United States has the largest Jewish population in the world and Jews have contributed greatly to all aspects of our society. Therefore, we have a personal stake in protecting communities as integral to the fabric of the United States. We need to work together with our European allies to combat anti-Semitism with the same vigor that we have with respect to protecting communities and to combating terrorism and ensuring peace and security around the world.

I look forward to working with my congressional colleagues, our European counterparts and the Jewish community all over the world to develop effective strategies to combat the rise of anti-Semitism in Europe and to work to ensure that this hatred is stopped in its tracks.

I thank you, Mr. Chairman.

Mr. SMITH. Thank you very much, Mr. Cicilline. Mr. Clawson.

Mr. CLAWSON. Thank you for coming today and sharing your personal stories.

Mr. Asmussen, I remember the sadness in my father's eyes when the murders took place in Denmark. Clawson is Danish. My forefathers come from about an hour south of Copenhagen in Borse in Zealand. My dad has taken me there. My father speaks Danish. And so it hit home to us personally and I will always remember his face when it happened. And he has told me he was glad his father wasn't here. So your words hit home and if there is anything that I can ever do, and I am sure my colleagues can ever do, to influence this in a positive way I am innately motivated to do so and see the innate unjustness of what is going on with the Jewish community in Europe.

I think of your question or your comment that the solution must come from within the Muslim community. That feels hopeful to me, but it also feels like we have to prepare for the fact that that might not happen. And if so, my question for the three of you then becomes what do we do next? What do we do now? Thank you.

Mr. SMITH. Thank you very much. Mr. Emmer?

Mr. EMMER. Well, I echo my colleagues' comments. I want to thank the chair for holding this important hearing and I just want to thank everyone, not only the witnesses, but everyone else who understands the importance of this issue and has taken time to be here today.

It is amazing how this place works. Things are planned all at the same time and typically the same committees, but that shouldn't be taken as we don't think this is important. This is of paramount importance. So my apologies for coming in late. My thanks to the chair for having this important hearing and for all of you being here. And let us say the discussion and the testimony and the issue needs to be at the forefront and we need to keep raising it so people understand they can't just ignore it. You need to call things what they are and you need to address them when they occur.

So again, thank you, Mr. Chair, and thank you to the witnesses.

Mr. SMITH. Mr. Emmer, thank you so very much as well. Let me begin the questioning if I could. At our hearing in February 2013, Zuhdi Jasser who is the President of the American Islamic Forum for Democracy and a very outspoken man in the combating of anti-Semitism made a very, very important insight, provided the committee a very important insight when he said, ''The link between Islamism and anti-Semitism is rather simple. It is self-evident that supremacists from within a particular faith community will create and exploit hatred toward another faith community in order to collectively rally their own followers against a common enemy.'' And then he went on to explain how this crowds out a more moderate Muslim view. And he said, ''These theo-fascists use the demonization of minorities as a populist tool to rally populations to their fanaticism.'' He went on in great depth and I will put part of this back into the record because I think it is so insightful that this is how they push out people—the Sadats of this world—who reach across and they divide and try to offer a common ground with Jews and with the State of Israel. And I am wondering what your thoughts might be on that because it seems as if the extremists win when there is not a counter force equal or greater to that effort.

Secondly, Mr. Asmussen, you mentioned Ira Forman. I would note for the record that in 2004, I sponsored the amendment that created that his office and position; very insightful at the time. Senator Voinovich had a bill that I sponsored on the House side. His bill passed, came over to the House. And I worked very closely with members on the other side of the aisle. We had a bipartisan effort to create an office that doesn't just do one report, but makes it permanent time and time again to do reports to monitor anti-Semitism and to create this position to work within the State Department as well. And I would appreciate your thoughts on how well you think that office might be doing. But at the time, 2004, Colin Powell, who was then Secretary of State, wrote a letter against the office, against the amendment. He thought the Human Rights bureau could handle the law. It was reminiscent of what Bill Clinton did when I offered the Trafficking Victims Protection Act, and it became law. He did sign it eventually, but the State Department sent over a letter saying, the Assistant Secretary for Democracy, Human Rights, and Labor, that they will just absorb all of this into the Human Rights Report and just do a little more reporting on it, but don't create a lane where this will be looked at for what it is.

Similarly, when we were working with the coalition and I formed it, of the willing, in the OSCE Parliamentary Assembly, I was shocked at how many members of Parliament said why don't we just expand it to everything. Now I do believe we need to combat anti-Christian beliefs and all the others. I have had hearings on it. What is happening, I know, Mr. Ambassador, you have spoken out very forcibly on that, but there is a specific sense of disproportionality to how Jews are singled out. Look at our own FBI statistics on hate crimes relative to belief, of faith. Christians far outnumber all other in the country, yet less than 10 percent of the FBI hate crimes are committed against Christians. Ditto for Muslims in this country. Not so for Jews who are the victims of over 60 percent of all the hate crimes, even though they are only 2 percent of the population.

It is so disproportionate. It cries out for a single focus. And even as we were doing the conferences, there is always this move by the Dutch and by others to just make it xenophobia, about other issues, always to exclude and in my opinion, reduce in its focus the issue of combating anti-Semitism. So your thoughts how Mr. Forman and how well you think that office is working.

I have other questions, but I want to make sure my colleagues get time to ask as well. So please, if you could begin.

Mr. ASMUSSEN. I believe, Congressman, Mr. Clawson asked me a question. I understand fully your skepticism toward getting the collective Muslim community in order to confront hate and prejudice. I understand it because what we see in Denmark and I talked to many Jewish leaders and it is the same all over. The Muslim community tends to be very fractured. You will never tend to find a body as we do within the Jewish community.

And I believe if we find racism and hate in Jewish community, we will confront it. The problem is it doesn't happen that often, but I see some changes. I mean sometimes you have to also look at the positive notes. And there are a few positive notes, mostly organizations, coming up with ideas like peace rings about synagogues. There are not many Muslims participating in these initiatives and I would not like to exaggerate. But there is a change.

So when you ask what is done now, there is a lot of things in Denmark being done by the government. After Paris, there was a huge catalogue of anti-terror legislation being rolled out. It seems like the murderer, he was known to the system. I mean he was—many people had reported him to the police intelligence again and again. He was released from jail 3 weeks before he killed. He went to authorities to get help getting a flat. No one did anything.

So there are a lot of things the community can do. You can do many things to spot radical behavior earlier. But also you can also do a lot and we are working on that in Denmark right now in order to spot and help people. But on the long term, nothing will change unless the mentality changes. If it is legitimate for religious leaders to teach hatred toward Jews, nothing will change. And we have cases in Denmark that imams have been doing exactly that and it takes a lot of time for the system to come down on them. So they keep on doing these things.

We are having organizations speaking intensely on hatred toward Jews, but it is very hard to outlaw them, according to Danish legislation. We are looking into it, but in my opinion in the long-term, the solution has to come from within.

Ambassador LAUDER. Mr. Chairman and members of the subcommittee, we are talking about Europe. Anti-Semitism is alive and well in this country. Starting off, it is taught. Children are born without hate. They are taught hate. It is most prevalent in universities, campuses. We have an organization called Caravan for Democracy which the Jewish National Fund does. We go on campuses all over. The amount of anti-Israel which morphs into anti-Jewish is happening all over. It is happening because there is an organized group putting money into these things to put pressure on Israel, but it goes into anti-Jewish also.

The media is guilty, very guilty. I watched CNN during the Gaza War. Ninety-five percent of it showed people in Gaza being killed. There was almost no coverage of the 4,000 rockets going to Israel. We watch it and it has an effect. And anti-Semitism is also learned at the dinner table. When a mother and father are sitting there and they watch television and they watch what happens and they see reporting that is so biased and they say to each other, look at those Jews what they are doing to people, look how they are killing people. Their children hear it and they repeat it. And what happened is that there was no understanding in media about what can be done.

We watch, we monitor what is happening on the Internet. It is disgusting what we see. And the amount of things that go on, and yet, there is no regulation against it. Anti-Semitism is going to morph into anti-Christian and anti-Muslim at times. We are at the beginning of something that is very, very dangerous, not only for Jews in Europe, but Jews throughout the world as well as Christians and for that matter, Muslims. We ask ourselves why aren't there more Muslim moderates? Because they are scared to death. If I was a Muslim and I was a moderate, I would be worried for my life because there is a feeling, it is not just we will vote and see who is right. There is a whole radical thing and it is taking over the country. It is taking over what is happening. And in many ways, what is happening in Europe is the canary in the mine. And the fact is that what is happening there will be happening here very shortly unless we react. And I commend the subcommittee for taking this up, but look at it not for Europe, not for Denmark, not for France, look at it for the world and look at it what is happening on our college campuses. There is something there.

We also see that in mosques the amount of hatred against Jews, but also against America there. We have monitored mosques and we see what is going on. A mosque is a place that should be for love and understanding. Too often, they are places of radicalism. We hear this. We know this. We have seen it. But the fact is there are no laws against it. There are no laws against what you can say and that is the danger. There is no law that what you can say on the Internet or media and we see it. We are just a small segment here.

You have 40 countries here. Each one country can sit here and testify what is happening here. We speak among ourselves and frankly, we feel powerless. I think if I asked every person what is the one place we look towards? We look toward the United States. We look toward the United States for the help and understanding because it is the one country that stands up for religious rights in a very strong way. We need the Congress. We need your help. We need people, not only this subcommittee, but a whole looking at what laws—you mentioned about Ira Forman, what went on. Here is one person that you tried to get in, you had people fighting it.

There is a feeling also that people don't want to see this. They want to stay away from it. We had a situation in California recently where a girl wanted to join an organization and because she was Jewish, was part of a Jewish organization, she was denied it. There should have been a huge outcry and there wasn't.

And again, Roger Cukierman is fighting a battle. He is fighting a battle. The French Government is there, but there is very little he can do. If you have 6 million Muslims, even if 1 percent of them, and using math without a computer, it is still 60,000 people who could be radical. What do you do about that? There are no laws about it.

Canada has just started to look at different laws that can be done. We must have type of things here in this country. It must be a chance for everybody to turn around and say this is the model. These are what should be done. And we are allowing it to happen.

Mr. CUKIERMAN. Yes, I want to say that anti-Semitism is not the problem of the Jews. It is the problem of the society. And it is not a European problem. It is a world problem. And we are in a war with jihadists. Jihadists are the fanatical Muslims and you were the first victims of that phenomenon on 9/11. I think 9/11 was the first step of that war. We are in a war and somebody asked among you what can you do? First of all, you have to realize that you are in a state of war. And secondly, you have to react at that state of war. One of the things which you can do is to see to it that the Internet stops being a school to educate jihadists.

Mr. SMITH. Thank you. Mr. Deutch.

Mr. DEUTCH. Thank you, Mr. Chairman, and thanks for giving me an opportunity just to sit in. I have another hearing. I appreciate it very much. Thanks for holding the hearing to you and Ranking Member Bass and thanks for your leadership on this and so many other human rights issues.

I appreciate the witnesses being here today, for offering their testimony. It is very helpful for Members of Congress to hear how the growth of anti-Semitism in recent years is viewed from a European perspective.

I will just make a couple of quick observations. We know that an overwhelming majority of the world's Jewish population lives in the United States and Israel, but in Europe where centuriess-old Jewish life was decimated by the Holocaust, the Jewish community that remains faces a growing animosity that is creating a very real security threat which your testimony here is so helpful to highlight. It is not to excuse, as Ambassador Lauder pointed out, it is not to excuse our own homegrown anti-Semitism. It certainly exists. The fact is it made up more than 50 percent of the religious bias-based hate crimes in 2013, but it is informative. It is helpful to hear how countries around the world are responding to intimidation tactics, to pressure, to deadly attacks on the Jewish populations.

The world as Ambassador Lauder said and as we have heard repeatedly and rightfully and importantly throughout your visit the past couple of days, the world has to take action because of what the rise of anti-Semitism means not just to the Jewish communities in Europe, but because of what the rise of anti-Semitism means to all countries that allow it to persist, what it actually portends for others.

And so I think we have to take action. I am proud to have joined with my colleagues, many of who are on the dais here today, the chairman in particular, to form the bipartisan task force for combating anti-Semitism, the purpose being we want to try to help our peers in Congress to understand the real and growing threat posed by anti-Semitism globally to allow Members of Congress to interact with the administration and to interact with NGOs and partners abroad to devise innovative ways to try to address these issues, to curb the threat and to attack it at its source.

And I will just finish, Mr. Chairman, by again highlighting that anti-Semitism matters to everyone. It is not just the Jews, but to every citizen in the world who values human rights. It is a shared threat. It is a threat that we have to work together to address what is our common problem.

And Ambassador Lauder, as you point out, efforts to mask anti-Semitism in some sort of anti-Israel rhetoric should be exposed for what they are. Ultimately, the threats posed by anti-Semitism are a threat, as I said, to all of us more broadly.

Your participation here, Mr. Chairman, your willingness to hold this hearing and your commitment to this issue means an enormous amount and I am grateful to be able to just stop by and participate. Thank you so much. I yield the rest of my time.

Mr. SMITH. Mr. Deutch, thank you very much for being here and for working in this issue so long and so hard yourself and we do have now, we have just revitalized and reconstituted a task force on combating anti-Semitism with four Republicans and four Democrats as co-chairs. We hope to invite frankly the entire House to join us. We have had this before, but I think having four co-chairs on each side will further demonstrate the significance of this commitment and that we really want to see action.

I do have questions I will ask a little bit later, but I would like to yield; we are joined by the gentleman from Arizona, Trent Franks, who is the chairman of the Constitution Subcommittee for the Judiciary Committee. He has been back and forth because he, too, has a markup going on. But he is also chairman of the Religious Freedom Caucus. So it is really a privilege to welcome him to the subcommittee.

Mr. FRANKS. Well, thank you, Mr. Chairman, and thanks to the subcommittee here for just allowing me the privilege to sit in on this. I am grateful to everyone that is here. I know that we have had anti-Semitism in the world for a long time, but it does seem like in recent days it has surged and I am incredibly discouraged about all of that.

My biggest fear is that somehow the countries of the world would somehow believe that America's commitment to Israel has diminished because that is of strategic significance to make it clear to the world that America is firmly with Israel and that Israel is with America. I am convinced that Israel is as important to America as America is to Israel. I know of no people on earth that contribute more to the cause of humanity than the people of Israel.

Mr. Chairman, it brings to my mind a quote by Shekh Hassan Nasrallah that really, I think, puts it into perspective. This is a jihadist that would do everything he could to destroy Israel if he could. And he said, ''You know, we have discovered how to hit the Jews where they are most vulnerable. The Jews love life. So that is what we shall take from them. We will win because they love life and we love death.'' Now that is a very frightening equation to face an enemy that loves death and is willing to embrace death in order to destroy another people based on just a bigoted point of view.

I would suggest to you, Mr. Chairman, that should be reason for great concern on the part of all us. The Jewish people have demonstrated a history that is unparalleled. when the Holocaust was over, if any people in the world had reason to quit, I suppose it was them, but instead of being crushed and instead of completely giving up, they got their revenge by living. They dried their eyes and looked up again and they began to build. And they built a community and they built a nation and today they are a force in the world for good and today, the Nazis are gone and Israel remains.

And Mr. Chairman, I think we need all be very committed to make sure that tomorrow, the jihadists will be gone and Israel will remain. I am grateful to you, sir, for this very valuable hearing. I think it is important that the world and the people of Israel know that some of their rhetoric that has come from our administration lately does not reflect the hearts of the Congress.

And with that, sir, I thank you for the opportunity.

Mr. SMITH. Thank you very much, Mr. Franks. Mr. Cicilline.

Mr. CICILLINE. Thank you, Mr. Chairman. Thank you again to our witnesses for your extraordinary testimony. My first question is I know there that are some who have observed that there is sort of an emergence of this kind of new normal, and Ambassador Lauder, you sort of made reference to this in the context of anti-Semitism. And that is the blurring of distinctions between being anti-Israel and anti-Jewish in which anti-Jewish remarks and sentiments are becoming more socially acceptable. And so I am wondering whether you think that is happening in Europe? What is your assessment of that?

And following that, one of the things that we are learning is that there is—some have written that there is a significant under reporting of incidents of anti-Semitism and that, of course, hampers our ability to kind of respond to it and help encourage people to craft responses to it. Do you think that it remains an issue, particularly in Europe and what can we do about that? That is my first question and maybe Ambassador Lauder, you could start.

Ambassador LAUDER. There is no question that the anti-Semitism starts as anti-Israel, no question. It is not in Europe. It is worldwide. And we hear it. We also have—yes, there is under reporting because very often when a child comes home from school and has been beaten up because he was Jewish, what is the mother going to do? Is she going to call the police and report it or she just says, ''Look, tomorrow, don't wear a yarmulke or take a different way.'' And the amount of unreporting is amazing. But also, I heard a couple of minutes ago about anti-Jewish and life and loving life. It is also anti-Christian. We look in the Middle East where there used to be Jews and the Jews left. Now there is almost no Christians left in the Middle East because of what is happening.

And the thing that we can't keep missing is that what is happening to the Jews is going to happen to everybody along the way, unless it is stopped. And the concern I have and the concern that I am delighted this subcommittee is here, is that we must do something more than either appoint somebody or have a hearing. We must start to look at what type of laws there are, what can be done, can we be a model? Can we stand up in the world?

There is no place like the United States to be able to stand up and do it. And countries should know that if they have things that are anti-Semitic, they have to pay a price, not only from the small Jewish communities, be it Denmark and many other countries don't have the strength to fight the government. The only chance they have is looking to the United States and looking to the United States as the model of where it goes.

I am sorry to be so passionate about it, but to me, what is happening in this world?

Mr. CUKIERMAN. I have an example of anti-Zionism turning to anti-Semitism. This summer, the period summer 2014 at the time of the Gaza War, there was a demonstration in Paris of 35,000 people in favor of the Palestinians, mostly Muslims. They didn't shout ''Death to Israel.'' They shouted, ''Death to the Jews.'' And from that demonstration went out hordes of people and they attacked eight synagogues and Jewish shops. What is the link if it is not anti-Zionism is anti-Semitism?

Mr. ASMUSSEN. I agree when you say there is somehow a presence of under reporting. Danish Jews basically stopped wearing yarmulkes many years ago. They don't dare. If they did, there are areas of Copenhagen as Mr. Lauder said, you will not be able to go without getting beaten up. So that is for sure there is under reporting.

In Denmark, we see primarily left wingers demonizing Israel. This tends to legitimize this hate toward Israel, toward Jews that is widespread within the Muslim minority.

Mr. CICILLINE. Could you speak to whether or not there has been countries that have been effective in either the EU or the EU itself in terms of responding to anti-Semitism that have implemented effective strategies? Are any of the countries doing it well? Is the Organization for Security and Co-operation in Europe doing anything? Are there things that the EU could be doing that they are not doing?

We have identified, I think, everyone understands this is a serious problem, but is there any——

Ambassador LAUDER. The closest I have heard is what Canada is doing and I have not seen yet, but I spoke to the Ambassador last night. He told me, the Canadian Ambassador, he told me some of the things they are doing. But to this day, they have not confronted it. It is fear. And you don't know how to confront it. How do you stop teaching of anti-Semitism in schools or in different mosques? How do you do it? And the question of freedom of speech, is there freedom of speech to be able to say in a mosque that the Jews are the bad people in the world? What are the laws on that? It is a very, very delicate thing. What are the laws on freedom of speech in the media when they report things one sided? What is the law in it? And it is a very, very dangerous thing. We do have laws now, very, very strong laws about segregation, what you can say against Blacks, but it is still a very, very difficult situation when it comes to Jewish things.

And also, I kept saying, it is going to come to Christians as well as Jews.

Mr. CICILLINE. I hope, Mr. Chairman, that one of the things that we can work on and I know the chairman is interested in this, because I do think you are right, so much of this has to do with education.

Ambassador LAUDER. Absolutely.

Mr. CICILLINE. And you look at kind of the early years, the formative years of so many young people. What are they learning? What are they being taught about people of different religious traditions and different cultures? Because I think as you said, Ambassador, this is taught. Nobody is born a bigot and nobody is born with this sort of hatred, but what can we do in terms of the assistance we provide and the programs that we fund to be sure that those resources aren't going to the teaching of young people to teach hate.

I think that we have a particular responsibility to do all that we can to promote understanding through good education. And I again thank you because I think as all the panelists pointed out, this is not only a problem in Europe, this is a problem all over the world and as that saying goes they begin and speaking against Jews and nobody says anything and they go down their groups. And this is about valuing the human life of every person and respecting differences and honoring and celebrating our diversity.

Can I ask with the indulgence one last question? Someone suggested that the rise of anti-Semitism, particularly in Europe, is closely connected to the sort of anti-immigration fervor. And I am wondering whether any of the panel have a view on that? And if so, what can be done about that?

Ambassador LAUDER. I can't say it is anti-immigration. That is a whole different thing. But it has to do very, very much with the times we are having. For example, the whole rise of Nazism came out of a very difficult financial time in Germany and Austria and all Europe for that matter. It gave rise to it.

We watched after 2008, the amount of anti-Semitism rose because once again as it happened for thousands of years, the Jews became the scapegoats. They looked at one—there was one case in Africa where there were three Jews and they were all wealthy. The amount of anti-Semitism in Africa, in that country was enormous because people look and say and it goes in jealously and what happens. But the fact is you have a confluence of bad economic times. You have a confluence of radical Islam growing leaps and bounds and you have a question of the media being able to feed this very, very much. And you have a question of the Palestinian-Israel question going on.

But I will say also that what happened during the last 2 or 3 weeks between Israel and the United States has had a marked effect on anti-Semitism because when people hear the fight between Israel and the United States, whatever it might be, it has an effect throughout the world of people saying even the best friend of Israel is having problems with them. That gives us the license to start talking also more and more negative.

Mr. CICILLINE. Before I yield back, Mr. Chairman, I think it is an important opportunity to say that while there might be disagreements between individuals or policies, I think it should be clear to everyone in the world that the relationship between our two countries is unbreakable. It is built on a set of shared values that will endure forever and I hope this hearing is an opportunity for us—I don't disagree with your conclusion.

Ambassador LAUDER. We all know that, but the world outside does not know that.

Mr. CICILLINE. I understand. Thank you.

Mr. MEADOWS [presiding]. And I thank the gentleman from Rhode Island for his passion and his willingness to work on this. I would echo what he just indicated. Headlines are headlines. Thirty-second sound bites, sixty-second sound bites, they sell media, but anybody who is watching this, they need to know that it is the foundation, the friendship, truly, the support both Democrat and Republican is unyielding and unwavering and as much as may be made out of that and running that abroad, I think you will find very quickly that there is a very unified effort to stand up for this particular cause. So I thank the gentleman for bringing it up.

Ambassador Lauder, I am going to go to you, first, and ask a very quick question. Maybe just a series and then recognize the gentleman from Minnesota that has a different accent than I do, Mr. Emmer.

Ambassador, one of the issues that you have been driving home is that America must lead on this particular issue and that when we don't, when we are silent, it has real implications in Europe and abroad, is that correct?

Ambassador LAUDER. That is correct.

Mr. MEADOWS. So if we are to be more than a hearing and more than just words, what is the most powerful way that we can show our support for the Jewish people? Because you know, it is interesting, Mr. Cukierman is talking about Zion versus being Jewish. I have never known anybody that hates a piece of land. And you know, when you really look at the Nation of Israel, it is really what it embodies that they hate versus really a geographical location. So what can we do?

Ambassador LAUDER. We can start talking about it, taking action ourselves, standing up, and saying for example, I gave the example of France and what happened. There was not one person that didn't notice that there was no American presence in that front line. And I must tell you that symbolism had a major effect on people.

It is important that we stand up, that we start talking about it and say there is no room for it. If there is a neo-Nazi party in a country, we must stand up and say that is unacceptable for that country.

If we see that there is anti-Semitic direction of a group, we must say that is unacceptable. That is not there. And I really believe the time is now.

Mr. MEADOWS. All right, Mr. Cukierman, how do we balance the line between free speech and truly standing up for hatred? It is a little known fact, I was born in France, actually, but I have been where there has been a number of demonstration, pro-Palestinian demonstrations in Paris and so how do we allow for this free speech, but yet not the results that may come from it?

Mr. CUKIERMAN. You have the example of pedophilia. The providers of Internet were able to fight against pedophilia very efficiently. Why don't they do the same for racism and anti-Semitism? Why don't they do the same against jihad? If they were able to do it for pedophilia, they should be able to do it because it is extremely important because today, this is the main school of education to the jihad.

Mr. MEADOWS. All right, so let me ask you maybe a little tougher question that you can weigh in on. The United States gives millions of dollars in foreign aid to a number of countries, most countries in some shape, form, or fashion. If incitement, and that is what I am hearing you talk about, really, it is more about incitement against the Jewish people. If incitement continues to be epidemic, should there be some tie to that foreign aid where we can get the attention? I will let you weigh in.

Mr. CUKIERMAN. I would not interfere into American policy, but what I noticed, for instance, is that the imams in France are usually paid by foreign countries. Among these foreign countries there are some countries who are financing Salafism.

Mr. MEADOWS. Right.

Mr. CUKIERMAN. Other countries are financing Muslim Brotherhood. Maybe America could put pressure on those countries which are friendly to the U.S. and see to it that they restrain their activity on fanaticism.

Mr. MEADOWS. Mr. Asmussen?

Mr. ASMUSSEN. When it comes to protecting Jewish minorities, I believe that the U.S. Government can also put political pressure on countries that are not taking these threats seriously. There are countries that take these threats very seriously and protects the Jewish minorities. There are countries that don't. And the political pressure from the outside from the United States, I believe, is very crucial.

There is some pressure by the World Jewish Congress, you mentioned Rabbi Andrew Baker, OSCE, and Ira Forman, but the U.S. Government can step up this political pressure.

Mr. MEADOWS. All right, thank you very much. I am going to close with this one story and then yield to the gentleman from Minnesota, Mr. Emmer.

I want to encourage each one of you. Ambassador Lauder, you talked about how the narrative during the Gaza conflict was one-sided. It was infuriating to me to see headline after headline after headline to be—and yet, I had on my phone an app that is called Red Alert. Many of you may have that on your phone and I got it. I was talking to the Ambassador one day, long before the conflict and it had gone on 42 times, I believe. This was at 11 o'clock in the morning. It was not being mentioned anywhere, no headlines, no nothing. And I asked the Ambassador, I said, "What is that?" And he said, "Well, it is an app that I have on my phone that is called Red Alert." I said, "Boy, I would love to have that, it would at least let me know when the missiles are coming in." He said, "Well, you can have it. The only problem is, it is in Hebrew."

Well, Hebrew is not a normal language in North Carolina and so we actually went to that. And had it translated and so it is on a number of Members' phones, a number of people I—I know there has been well over 1 million downloads. And so I would encourage you as something to be a reminder. Because even as recent as January, there were missiles going into Israel and it is important that we do that. And so I thank you because we have got to change the narrative, Ambassador.

I am going to recognize the gentleman from Minnesota, Mr. Emmer.

Mr. EMMER. Thank you, Mr. Chair. A couple of questions. I will try not to cover old ground. The first one and I think what I will do is start with Mr. Cukierman.

Can you outline for me, briefly, what measures the Jewish communities in France are taking for their physical safety right now? We have heard testimony and I am aware that there are some resources that have been deployed, but what are the communities themselves doing to protect themselves?

Mr. CUKIERMAN. We are first of all an organization which the volunteers are protecting the Jewish places, the synagogues and

Jewish schools mainly. But this has been strongly reinforced recently by the government because our protectors are not armed. They are just checking that the people who went to Jewish places are not suspicious. But this is the main thing and we also tried to have organizations which it is not easy to enter. We have videos. It is defense. It is not efficient.

I must say that we are very satisfied of the attitude of the French Government in the recent events. I am not generally putting compliments to the French Government. I have frequently criticized from my past reactions. But in these difficult periods, they have been exemplary. The Prime Minister has said very strong words like anti-Zionist is anti-Semitism and the President said that it is not the Jews who should leave, but it is the anti-Semites.

And the day which followed the January event, we had immediately the Army who joined the police to protect Jewish places. So we don't have to complain about protection. The legislation is a prominent in terms of fighting against anti-Semitism. For instance, Holocaust denial is a crime in France which is not the case in other countries. So the laws are satisfactory. The main problem would be education because today in public schools Jews are not going any more because the atmosphere has become so much anti-Semitic that people prefer to pay and go to private schools, either Jewish schools or Christian schools, rather than public schools.

Mr. EMMER. Yes, but then the problem is not being addressed apparently in the public schools or is it?

Mr. CUKIERMAN. Nothing has been done in terms of education in public schools in the last 30 years and there we are terribly backwards.

Mr. EMMER. Mr. Asmussen, same question. What are the Jewish communities doing in Denmark since the incidents to protect themselves?

Mr. ASMUSSEN. Basically after the attacks in Toulouse and Brussels, Brussels was last summer, we contacted the Danish Ministry of Justice in order for them to improve security around Jewish institutions. Nothing happened. There is security. There are roundings in police cars and we have as in France, our voluntary security guards within the community. But we asked for armed police in front of the synagogue during services, in front of the Jewish school when the kids are there. We didn't get it. We didn't get it because it was not on the menu in Denmark. Denmark is a small, peaceful country. You don't have policemen on the street wearing guns. Now we do.

As in France, it takes people getting killed before they get the message. But what we see now, I believe in France and in Denmark might not be the long-term solution and basically it is too much right now. I have a school of 200 pupils with eight policemen with machine guns. It is too much. But I need a long-term solution on that issue with the government. I don't have it at this point.

So now I say what can I do? I tell you what the government can do. But we are trying to put pressure on the government. And in the long run, of course, we can participate in education, learning about Judaism, of course. We can intensify our activities within the interfaith, with Christians, Muslim, interfaith activities as we do.

But somehow it seems that all those interfaith activities seems to be together with the people with the politically correct minds, not the people doing all the anti-Semitic activities.

Mr. EMMER. We have a bit of that in this country as well.

Mr. Lauder, and thank you for that. In Minnesota, the chairman referenced the accent. We have a phrase, I don't know that I want to open this can of worms, but I think I am going to. We are talking about what the Congress might help with, what this country might help with, what we could do. What about the organization known as the United Nations?

Ambassador LAUDER. It is a joke.

Mr. EMMER. I am going to open that can of worms. If you could just give an idea. Is the United Nations a lost cause when it comes to this? Is there something that can be done through that organization?

Ambassador LAUDER. Of the 25 recent cases of attacks on what should be done in religion, 23 were against Israel. The United Nations is perhaps one of the most anti-Israel, anti-Jewish organizations there.

Mr. EMMER. Can I ask a question that is very direct? The response or lack thereof by the United Nations, does that also fuel in your opinion of an increase in anti-Semitism?

Ambassador LAUDER. Everything fuels it. The real question is if you have a case where one country, if Canada attacked Minnesota with 4,000 rockets and you responded and all of a sudden they took Minnesota to the International Criminal Court for what you did to protect yourself, how would you feel? And the International Criminal Court, I believe, has something to do with the United Nations. That is a symbol of what is happening.

And we spoke before about UNRWA and the fact that Palestinians are still receiving refugee status where the 800,000 people who left the Middle East and came to Israel and things like that, don't get refugee status. It is a dual standard that goes on and on. It is something that I know that the committee knows very, very well. The real aspect is this is something that has been anti-Semitism since almost right after Abraham. It is something that we have seen all the time.

What has happened recently is that anti-Semitism has started to kill people, has started to become radicalization and it is one group of people who are doing it and the world is turning its back on it and not really necessarily going after it.

Mr. EMMER. And I will be done, Mr. Chair, but I think you made the point and it was an artful answer. When everyone——

Ambassador LAUDER. It was a diplomatic answer.

Mr. EMMER. Very diplomatic answer and I do appreciate it and respect it. But if our institutions that are there, I mean we are talking about the media on one hand and there is an issue with education in sensitivity and awareness. But when the very institutions that are created to promote peace and to try and help resolve conflict, actually don't do that. In fact, by their actions, some could interpret it as fueling the conflict. It is not very helpful and I don't know if that is the case, but that is what I was asking.

Ambassador LAUDER. That is the case.

Mr. EMMER. Thank you.

Mr. MEADOWS. I thank the gentlemen. I thank each of you for your testimony here today. Chairman Smith actually is monitoring this, his staff is monitoring it. He has been having a few health issues. We will support and actually give some questions for each one of you that you can respond in writing for the record. I would also ask each of you if you have two recommendations on what you would like to see the United States to do, if you would just submit that to the committee, we will make sure that that gets passed around and we will take action on that.

And so I want to close out by saying there are many times when this battle may seem like we are losing the battle and indeed many battles have been lost. But ultimately, the victory in the war will be ours if we continue to fight arm in arm and stand arm in arm together. I for one, and I know a number of my colleagues are willing to do that so thank you for your testimony. Thank you for being here. God bless. This is adjourned.

[Whereupon, at 4:23 p.m., the subcommittee was adjourned.]

APPENDIX

Material Submitted for the Record

SUBCOMMITTEE HEARING NOTICE
COMMITTEE ON FOREIGN AFFAIRS
U.S. HOUSE OF REPRESENTATIVES
WASHINGTON, DC 20515-6128

Subcommittee on Africa, Global Health, Global Human Rights, and International Organizations
Christopher H. Smith (R-NJ), Chairman

March 24, 2015

TO: MEMBERS OF THE COMMITTEE ON FOREIGN AFFAIRS

You are respectfully requested to attend an OPEN hearing of the Committee on Foreign Affairs, to be held by the Subcommittee on Africa, Global Health, Global Human Rights, and International Organizations in Room 2175 of the Rayburn House Office Building (and available live on the Committee website at http://www.ForeignAffairs.house.gov):

DATE: Tuesday, March 24, 2015

TIME: 2:30 p.m.

SUBJECT: After Paris and Copenhagen: Responding to the Rising Tide of Anti-Semitism

WITNESSES: The Honorable Ronald S. Lauder
President
World Jewish Congress

Mr. Roger Cukierman
President
Representative Council of Jewish Institutions of France

Mr. Dan Rosenberg Asmussen
President
Danish Jewish Community

By Direction of the Chairman

The Committee on Foreign Affairs seeks to make its facilities accessible to persons with disabilities. If you are in need of special accommodations, please call 202/225-5021 at least four business days in advance of the event, whenever practicable. Questions with regard to special accommodations in general (including availability of Committee materials in alternative formats and assistive listening devices) may be directed to the Committee.

COMMITTEE ON FOREIGN AFFAIRS

MINUTES OF SUBCOMMITTEE ON _Africa, Global Health, Global Human Rights, and International Organizations_ HEARING

Day____ _Tuesday_____ Date____ _March 24, 2015_____ Room _2175 Rayburn HOB_

Starting Time ____ _2:43 p.m._____ Ending Time ____ _4:24 p.m._

Recesses |___ _0_ ___| (____to ____) (____to ____) (____to ____) (____to ____) (____to ____) (____to ____)

Presiding Member(s)

Rep. Chris Smith, Rep. Mark Meadows

Check all of the following that apply:

Open Session ☑
Executive (closed) Session ☐
Televised ☑

Electronically Recorded (taped) ☑
Stenographic Record ☑

TITLE OF HEARING:

After Paris and Copenhagen: Responding to the Rising Tide of Anti-Semitism

SUBCOMMITTEE MEMBERS PRESENT:

Rep. David Cicilline, Rep. Curt Clawson, Rep. Tom Emmer

NON-SUBCOMMITTEE MEMBERS PRESENT: _(Mark with an * if they are not members of full committee.)_

Rep. Trent Franks*, Rep. Theodore Deutch

HEARING WITNESSES: Same as meeting notice attached? Yes ☑ No ☐
(If "no", please list below and include title, agency, department, or organization.)

STATEMENTS FOR THE RECORD: _(List any statements submitted for the record.)_

Statement of Rep. Eliot Engel, submitted by Rep. Chris Smith
Statement of Dr. Zuhdi Jasser, submitted by Rep. Chris Smith
Statement of the Anti-Defamation League, submitted by Rep. Chris Smith

TIME SCHEDULED TO RECONVENE _____
or
TIME ADJOURNED ____ _4:24 p.m._

Gregory B. Simpkins
Subcommittee Staff Director

MATERIAL SUBMITTED FOR THE RECORD BY THE HONORABLE CHRISTOPHER H. SMITH, A REPRESENTATIVE IN CONGRESS FROM THE STATE OF NEW JERSEY, AND CHAIRMAN, SUBCOMMITTEE ON AFRICA, GLOBAL HEALTH, GLOBAL HUMAN RIGHTS, AND INTERNATIONAL ORGANIZATIONS

Eliot Engel, Ranking Member, House Committee on Foreign Affairs
Opening Statement for Subcommittee on Africa, Global Human Rights, Global Health and International Organizations hearing *"After Paris and Copenhagen: Responding to the Rising Tide of Anti-Semitism"*
March 24, 2015

I want to thank the Chairman and Ranking Member for holding this important hearing.

Let me also thank the witnesses for joining us today. It's no secret that anti-Semitism is once again rearing its ugly head all over the world, particularly in Europe. We look forward to your views on the situations in France, in Denmark, and on the continent as a whole. I also want to express my deepest condolences to your communities for the tragedies they have suffered.

As the Ranking Member of the House Foreign Affairs Committee and the Chairman of the International Council of Jewish Parliamentarians, I am doing everything in my power to fight anti-Semitism worldwide. And the United States and governments around the world need to meet this challenge with a strong and united front.

This current wave of anti-Semitism is being dressed up as opposition to the policies of Israel—the only reliable democracy in the Middle East. But what does killing Jews in a kosher grocery store or their places of worship have anything to do with Israel?

The answer, of course, is "nothing." Anti-Semitism has been around much longer than the state of Israel and anti-Semites simply use Israeli policy to justify their hatred.

Just a few months ago the Anti-Defamation League released the results of a survey on global anti-Semitic attitudes. It found that more than one-quarter of those surveyed, 26 percent, harbor anti-Semitic attitudes. That statistic represents more than a billion adults around the world.

Only 54 percent of those polled globally have ever heard of the Holocaust. Two out of three people surveyed have either never heard of the Holocaust, or do not believe historical accounts are accurate. These are troubling and dangerous findings.

Anti-Semitism has also found its way back in to European politics, and often times, these parties affect Jews and other minorities. The Jobbik Party in Hungary openly uses Nazi style rhetoric, ideology, and anti-Semitism to push its right-wing nationalistic agenda of hatred. Greece's Golden Dawn Party, which is more like a criminal outlet than a political party, has been accused by both the Greek public and Greek leadership of using anti-Semitism as part of its anti-immigrant fervor. And just last year, the Danish government passed legislation that effectively banned kosher and halal slaughter practices. While perhaps not intended to be malicious, it is nonetheless an assault on the religious freedom of both Jewish and Muslim communities.

But even as we mourn the dead and confront those responsible for these bigoted and heinous crimes, we draw inspiration from the displays of courage and solidarity on the streets across Europe, and around the world. While the attackers in Paris were still at large, Parisians took to the streets in massive and peaceful vigils. They sent a clear message to the world that freedom and justice will not be cowed by violence and terror. In Denmark, hundreds of Muslims, Jews, and Christians formed a human ring outside the synagogue in Copenhagen as a sign of unity that everyone should be able to practice their religion freely and safely.

These are difficult times. And they require our unwavering vigilance and compassion. We must continue to work hard and work together to battle anti-Semitism. Thank you again Mr. Chairman and Mr. Ranking Member for holding this important hearing, and thank you again to our witnesses for joining us today.

MATERIAL SUBMITTED FOR THE RECORD BY THE HONORABLE CHRISTOPHER H. SMITH, A REPRESENTATIVE IN CONGRESS FROM THE STATE OF NEW JERSEY, AND CHAIRMAN, SUBCOMMITTEE ON AFRICA, GLOBAL HEALTH, GLOBAL HUMAN RIGHTS, AND INTERNATIONAL ORGANIZATIONS

TESTIMONY OF
M. ZUHDI JASSER, M.D.
PRESIDENT, AMERICAN ISLAMIC FORUM FOR DEMOCRACY
February 27, 2013

U.S. House of Representatives, Committee on Foreign Affairs, Subcommittee on Africa, Global Health, Global Human Rights, and International Organizations

"Anti-Semitism: A Growing Threat to All Faiths"

Thank you Chairman Christopher Smith and Ranking Member Karen Bass, and distinguished members of the committee, for seeking my testimony. I must first express my gratitude to the committee for taking the time to focus on the issue of anti-Semitism and its important role as a 'canary in the coal mine', if you will, for the threat against all people and all faiths.

My name is Dr. M. Zuhdi Jasser and I am the president and founder of the American Islamic Forum for Democracy. Our organization's mission is the advancement of our Constitution's principles of freedom and liberty through the separation of mosque and state. As a Muslim organization we are particularly focused upon the need to generate a consensus of reform against the ideas of political Islam and the Islamic state vis-à-vis the promotion of the ideas of liberty and pluralism.

On behalf of our organization I have written and testified repeatedly in these halls about the threat of Islamist extremism and the need for our society to identify, understand, dissect, counter and then defend against the ideology that threatens us. Different from many "politically correct" approaches to this issue I have not found the nebulous and generic concept of "violent extremism" particularly helpful in developing targeted solutions against this domestic and global threat. Programs that only counter violence address the *means* of those who threaten us while wholly ignoring the ideology or the *ends* which their movements seek. The common ideological thread which runs through the security threat that comes from Islamist extremism is the inherent supremacism of Islamism or political Islam. Thus, violent extremism is but one threatening symptom or manifestation that comes out of the Islamist ideology that threatens western democracies and citizenry under its sway.

The Link between Anti-Semitism and Islamism

Anti-Semitism should not be viewed as just another "radical" symptom that arises from the supremacist mentality of Islamism. It is far more than that. If we can develop the understanding and national conviction to directly confront the anti-Semitism of global Islamist movements, we will therein hold the key to unraveling the very fabric and platform through which Islamist leaders spread their ideas. The Helsinki Commission and the members of your committee have a rich history of being fearless in seeking to shed the anti-septic of the light of day upon anti-Semitism in Europe and the West wherever it exists in order to preserve the essence of our democracies and prevent us from abandoning the central premise of the equality of all under God, blind to faith or no faith. The need to do the same with anti-Semitism that arises and metastasizes from the propaganda of Islamist movements around the world has never been greater than it is today.

The link between Islamism and anti-Semitism is rather simple. It is self-evident that supremacists from within a particular faith community will create and exploit hatred towards another faith community in order to collectively rally their own followers against a common enemy. Islamists utilize anti-Semitic imagery, profiling and demonization of Jews as a tool for their own ascension into power among Muslim majority communities and nations, or in Arabic, the "*Ummah*". Islamists often exploit both the Muslim *Ummah* and the Jewish minority in order to create a groupthink against the "other". The demonization of Jews by

 Testimony of M. Zuhdi Jasser, MD, U.S. House of Representatives Committee on Foreign Affairs Subcommittee on Africa, Global Health, Global Human Rights, and International Organizations, "Anti-Semitism: A Growing Threat to All Faiths"

Islamists is a key signal to all of us not only because of its imminent threat to all Jews across the world from Islamists who may become violent or oppressive, but also because beneath that hatred lies a more global supremacism that treats all minorities from within the faith and outside the same as obstacles to their own ascension. These theo-fascists use the demonization of minorities as populist tools to rally populations to their fascism.

Understanding this inextricable link between the demonization of Jews or anti-Semitism and the advancement of Islamist movements is essential to how our nation approaches finding the keys that will unlock and unravel the threat of Islamism domestically and abroad.

While addressing "violent extremism" has given many a pass in dealing with the faith-based component of the societal and political threat of Islamism, the spread of anti-Semitism by Islamists does not. It is the Jewish faith group that is being attacked and demonized and I, as a devout American Muslim, have dedicated my life to countering the Islamist demagogues and their ideas from within our faith community that target Jews. Those ideas could never be targeted without acknowledging the role of political Islam and the Islamic state ascendancy in creating a fertile soil for anti-Semitism. It is in defense of our Constitution, the Universal Declaration of Human Rights and in my own enlightened self-interest as a Muslim that I sit before you and pray that you join us in understanding the need to develop a national strategy against Islamism in order to begin to eliminate anti-Semitism across the globe.

The Arab Awakening: Islamism rushes to fill the vacuum, anti-Semitism led the way

Europe and the West are being directly impacted by the events of the last two years during the Arab Awakening. With the tumult in Libya, Egypt, Tunisia, Yemen, Bahrain and Syria, the ascent of Islamist movements has not brought a real spring but rather the empowerment of new autocrats who wield Islamist thought. To many, the Islamist movements are simply dictators on theocratic steroids. With vast global connections in Arabic social and traditional media, Muslim populations in Europe and the United States are being impacted by a great deal of the propaganda coming out of these regions now with unleashed Islamist movements.

The new-found avenues of public discourse (Facebook, Twitter and YouTube) and attempts at media freedom are long overdue for the region which has been crushed by generations of unforgiving dictatorship. However, whether they are truly moving towards more transparent societies with actual checks and balances of a genuinely free media remains to be seen. The reality on the ground is that media and thought has been dominated for quite some time by extraordinarily wealthy Islamist media arms like, *Al Jazeera Media Group* (funded by the Emir and government of Qatar), the Kingdom of Saudi Arabia (and its royal family) and the Iranian government (Khomeinists) to name just a few of the wealthy benefactors of Islamist movements. In fact, recent reports are that in Egypt, for example, while the revolution was driven by greater grass roots social media freedoms, the Muslim Brotherhood now in power is buckling down on free speech in ways that are even worse than they were under Mubarak. Arrests for blasphemy and criticism of the President are dwarfing what they were in the previous years. Heba Morayef of Human Rights Watch in Egypt stated, *"The repression used to be more limited and strategic, now, the scary thing is that it's all over the place."*[1]

To many of us, the anti-Semitism of the Muslim Brotherhood's Islamist ideology was long a harbinger of what to expect if Islamists ever came to power. Their anti-freedom, neo-theocratic methods are part and parcel of the same supremacist ideology. Interestingly, Islamist groups in the West, those created in the late 20th century as Muslim Brotherhood legacy groups have not demonstrably utilized the opportunity of the Arab Awakening to push forth reforms against neo-theocratic institutions and ideologies. Instead, they are

---

[1] Cambannis, Thannasis. Egypts' free-speech backlash: What can you say in an Islamist democracy? A new conflict that could reverberate across the Muslim world. The Boston Globe. February 10, 2013.

 Testimony of M. Zuhdi Jasser, MD, U.S. House of Representatives Committee on Foreign Affairs Subcommittee on Africa, Global Health, Global Human Rights, and International Organizations, "Anti-Semitism: A Growing Threat to All Faiths"

being told by European and American Islamist demagogues like Tariq Ramadan[2] to 'learn from the Egyptians' about how to fight back against their own governments. Ramadan, the grandson of Hassan Al-Banna founder of the Muslim Brotherhood, told thousands at the annual *Reviving the Islamic Spirit* conference in Toronto December 2012 that they should take a lesson from Egypt, *"and be courageous enough to say "no" when there are injustices...done to the Muslims in the jails, innocent people suspected of being connected to so called terrorist organizations."*[3] Thus, contrary to genuine anti-Islamist Muslim reformers in Muslim communities, Islamists and their sympathizers in the West obsessively focus upon blaming the West, or "the other", for the "Muslim condition" and constantly pit Muslim communities in the West against "non-Muslim" governments. This is a natural sequel to the history of indoctrination with the divisive mantra of anti-Semitism and its conspiracy laden philosophies.

Yet, sadly virtually nothing is said to Muslim audiences in the West by Muslim leaders especially of Islamist legacy groups about the central need to combat the institutional ideas of anti-Semitism. Some have even featured anti-Semitic speakers at their national conventions.[4]

The challenge before the world could not be clearer — into the abyss left by ruthless dictators is a widening front in the battle for the soul of Islam: Will Muslim majority societies and Muslim leaders around the world heed the call of the Arab spring for the rights of the individual? Will they defend the rights of the minority over the collective, over the tribe, over the clerical oligarchs? Or will they just trade one autocracy for another? And will the U.S. and the West stand on the principles we were founded upon?

New ideas to the region like individual liberty and the separation of mosque and state are not turned on like a light switch. They are nurtured in a soil that has been tilled for critical thinking. Middle Eastern soil today is far from that. What we see today is more of the past battles between the evils of secular Arab fascism and theocratic fascism. In the information war between them, the liberals and secular democrats have been absent. Meanwhile, the fascists lie in wait for openings like a controversial film or cartoons that exploit the imagined threat or conspiracy of American imperialism in order to legitimize their own ascendancy. That is the demagogic role that anti-Semitism takes on too easily in the vacuum of the departure of secular Arab fascists. We have for too long left untended the war of ideas for liberty and individual rights within Muslim majority nations and communities, especially those now undergoing upheavals screaming for help of liberals. We have refused to take sides within the theo-political debates going on inside the Muslim communities at the expense of so many minority victims of Islamists, like the Jewish community, in the face of rampant and endemic anti-Semitism. This is to our own peril.

The importance of the role of anti-Semitism here cannot be overstated. Both in Tunisia and in Egypt the Islamist parties received only a plurality of the vote in the first balloting, but due to fractionalization and division, the secularists and non-Islamists were never able to rally around any unifying idea that could have marginalized the Islamists. In fact, anti-Semitism was long a tool utilized by Islamists in order to invoke common sympathy from secular nationalists, who also developed a hatred for Jews, in order to avoid national introspection.

Follow the numbers: first anti-Semitism then Islamism's fascism

Even though in Egypt, the Islamists carried only 25 percent support among the population and the more extreme salafists carried 15-20 percent, Pew revealed that "Anti-Jewish sentiment" is endemic in the Muslim world. *"In Lebanon, for example, all Muslims and 99% of Christians say they have a very unfavorable view of Jews. Similarly, 99% of Jordanians have a very unfavorable view of Jews. Large majorities of Moroccans,*

---

[2] Fourest, Caroline. *Brother Tariq: The Doublespeak of Tariq Ramadan.* Encounter Books. London. 2008
[3] Ramadan, Tariq. In the absence of the Caliph: Muslims in Pluralistic Societies, Video of speech on Halaltube. (accessed February 25, 2013).
[4] Mainstream Islamist convention features hate speech and Hizballah defense. Investigative Project on Terrorism. July 8, 2009

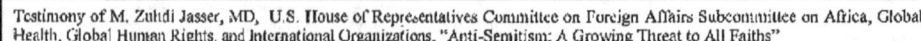

Testimony of M. Zuhdi Jasser, MD, U.S. House of Representatives Committee on Foreign Affairs Subcommittee on Africa, Global Health, Global Human Rights, and International Organizations, "Anti-Semitism: A Growing Threat to All Faiths"

For the complete version of this document, please access Dr. Jasser's statement at
http://foreignaffairs.house.gov/hearing/subcommittee-hearing-anti-semitism-growing-threat-all-faiths

MATERIAL SUBMITTED FOR THE RECORD BY THE HONORABLE CHRISTOPHER H. SMITH, A REPRESENTATIVE IN CONGRESS FROM THE STATE OF NEW JERSEY, AND CHAIRMAN, SUBCOMMITTEE ON AFRICA, GLOBAL HEALTH, GLOBAL HUMAN RIGHTS, AND INTERNATIONAL ORGANIZATIONS

Statement by the Anti-Defamation League

to the Subcommittee on Africa, Global Health, Global Human Rights, and International Organizations Hearing:

After Paris and Copenhagen: Responding to the Rising Tide of Anti-Semitism

March 24, 2015

We commend Chairman Smith, Ranking Member Bass, and the Members of the House Foreign Affairs Subcommittee on Africa, Global Health, Global Human Rights, and International Organizations for holding today's hearing on global anti-Semitism.

Today's hearing is entitled "After Paris and Copenhagen: Responding to the Rising Tide of Anti-Semitism." We must remember, however, that before Paris and Copenhagen, there were the terror attacks by Islamic extremists in May 2014 at the Jewish Museum of Brussels and at the Jewish school in Toulouse in March 2012.

The alarms have been ringing loudly for years. Terror attacks against Jewish targets grab the headlines, but insecurity in Jewish communities has been at high levels for years.

A 2013 survey of European Jewish communities by the European Union's Fundamental Rights Agency revealed tremendous insecurity. Almost half of the respondents worried about being insulted or harassed in public for being Jewish, and a third worried about becoming the victim of a physical assault because they were Jewish. Three quarters responded that anti-Semitism had increased over the past five years. And that was before Paris, Copenhagen, and Brussels.

Several factors affect the confidence level of Jews to live openly and freely as Jews, and those factors differ in emphasis in different communities. The Jewish communities in France and Hungary are both under significant threat, for instance, but the threats themselves differ significantly. These differ from, for example, South Africa or Argentina.

The main factors relating to anti-Semitism are: (1) the degree of anti-Semitic attitudes held by the general population; (2) the number and nature of anti-Semitic incidents; (3) anti-Semitism in politics and media; and (4) the reaction of governments and civil society to those incidents.

What is Anti-Semitism?

Anti-Semitism is a form of hatred, mistrust, and contempt for Jews based on a variety of stereotypes and myths, and often invokes the belief that Jews have extraordinary influence with which they conspire to harm or control society. It can target Jews as individuals, as a group or a people, or it can target Israel as a Jewish entity. Criticism of Israel or Zionism is anti-Semitic when it uses anti-Jewish stereotypes or invokes anti-Semitic symbols and images, or holds Jews collectively responsible for actions of the State of Israel. Appended to this statement is a brief description of anti-Semitism and the manifestations we are seeing today. Appendix I of this statement notes the key themes of contemporary anti-Semitism, and Appendix II outlines select incidents that exemplify some of the trends discussed below.

Attitudes

In May 2014, the Anti-Defamation League ("ADL") released an unprecedented worldwide survey of anti-Semitic attitudes (global100.adl.org). *The ADL Global 100: An Index of Anti-Semitism* surveyed 53,100 adults in 102 countries and territories in an effort to establish, for the first time, a comprehensive data-based research survey of the level and intensity of anti-Jewish sentiment across the world.

The survey found that anti-Semitic attitudes are persistent and pervasive around the world. More than one in four adults, 26% of those surveyed, are deeply infected with anti-Semitic attitudes. This figure represents an estimated 1.09 billion people around the world.

The overall ADL Global 100 Index score represents the percentage of respondents who answered "probably true" to six or more of 11 negative stereotypes about Jews.

The highest concentration of respondents holding anti-Semitic attitudes was found in Middle East and North African countries ("MENA"), where nearly three-quarters of respondents, 74 % of those polled, agreed with a majority of the anti-Semitic stereotypes that comprise the 11-question index. Non-MENA countries have an average index score of 23%.

Outside MENA, the index scores by region were as follows:

- Eastern Europe: 34%
- Western Europe: 24%
- Sub-Saharan Africa: 23%
- Asia: 22%
- The Americas: 19%
- Oceania: 14%

The 18 countries/entities surveyed in MENA demonstrated a high level of anti-Semitic sentiment, and an overwhelming acceptance of anti-Semitic conspiracy theories. The West Bank and Gaza Strip (98%) and Iraq (92%) had the highest index scores. Iran, interestingly, had the lowest in the region at 56%. Of the 102 countries/entities we surveyed, the 16 with the highest Index scores are all from MENA. Also troubling is that only 38% in MENA have heard about the Holocaust, compared to 94% in Western Europe and 24% in Sub-Saharan Africa. Of those who have heard about the Holocaust, in MENA, only 8% believe it has been accurately described by history, making it the lowest scoring region.

Another interesting anomaly in MENA concerns education. In much of the world, the more educated a person is, the less likely they are to harbor anti-Semitic views. In MENA, the more educated people are, the more likely they are to hold anti-Semitic views.

It is important to note that regional tends to be a stronger factor than religion in determining anti-Semitic attitudes. For example, the average Index score for MENA is 74%. Muslims overall have the highest average Index score, 49%, of all religions tested, but they vary significantly among regions: 75% in MENA, 37% in Asia, and 29% in Western Europe. Christians in MENA have higher average Index scores than those in other regions of the world: 64% in MENA, compared to 35% in Eastern Europe and 25% in Western Europe.

Among the lowest scores of those surveyed are Laos (0.2%) and the Philippines (3%). Interestingly, levels of anti-Semitic attitudes are particularly low in English-speaking countries, with only 13% of people living in English-speaking countries harboring anti-Semitic attitudes, half the worldwide average.

Several European Union ("EU") states were among the lowest scorers in the world. Sweden (4%), the Netherlands (5%), and the United Kingdom (8%) all scored better than the United States (9%), and Denmark tied.

Other EU states had disappointing scores: France (37%), Hungary (41%), Bulgaria (44%), Poland (45%), and Greece with an astounding 69%, making it the worst-scoring country in the world outside the Middle East and North Africa.

In Latin America, Spanish speaking countries had an average index score of 31%, compared to 19% of all the Americas. Of all countries in the Americas, Panama had the highest score, 52%, and ranked 24th in the entire survey. Brazil had the lowest score in Latin America, 16%, and Argentina and Mexico tied at 24%.

Incidents

There is a massive data deficit on anti-Semitic incidents, because the majority of countries do not monitor, document, and publicize anti-Semitic hate crimes as a separate category in police records.

Only nine of the 28 EU member states published data on anti-Semitic crimes: Austria, Czech Republic, France, Germany, Ireland, Poland, Spain, Sweden, and the United Kingdom.

Compounding the problem is massive under-reporting of incidents by the victims themselves. The EU survey showed 76% of victims of anti-Semitic harassment did not report the incident to police or to a Jewish organization. Even more startling, 64% of victims of physical violence did not go to the police or to a Jewish organization.

The data we do have from France and the United Kingdom ("UK") indicate severe problems with anti-Semitic violence, especially compared to the United States.

While vandalism and harassment discourage communities, physical violence is of utmost concern. Comparing the numbers of violent anti-Semitic incidents for 2008-2014 in the UK, France and the United States ("U.S.") demonstrates how different the experience of American Jews is from the experiences of British and French Jews.

In France, per 100,000 Jews, there were 15 assaults per year over that seven year period. In the UK, there were 31 assaults per 100,000 Jews per year. In the US, ADL's annual Audit of Anti-Semitic Incidents reported an annual average of just 0.4 assaults per 100,000 Jews.

For the complete version of this document, please access Support Document #2 at
http://docs.house.gov/Committee/Calendar/ByEvent.aspx?EventID=103237

3

www.ingramcontent.com/pod-product-compliance
Lightning Source LLC
Chambersburg PA
CBHW080912290526
45795CB00007BA/2510